Country houses

Country houses

THE ARTS OF THE HABITAT

Series directed by Olivier Boissière

Front cover
Frank O. Gehry.
House in Wayzata,
United States.

Back cover
Charles Gwathmey
and Robert Siegel.
House in East
Hampton, New York,
United States.

Preceding page
Often zoomorphic in style,
houses by American
architect Bart Prince are
always sumptuous.

Publisher editor: Jean-François Gonthier
Art director: Bruno Leprince
Cover design: Daniel Guerrier
Editing staff: Catherine Donzel, Charles-Arthur Boyer, Christian Pottgiesser
Translation: Unity Woodman
Assistant to the publisher: Sophie-Charlotte Legendre
Correction and revision: Jack Monet
Composition: Graffic, Paris
Filmsetting: Compo Rive Gauche, Paris
Lithography: ARCO Editorial, Barcelone

This edition copyright © TELLERI, PARIS 1998
All illustrations copyright © ARCO Editorial except for the cover
ISBN : 2-7450-0006-3
Printed in Italy

RETRO COOL

To the uninitiated, Barbara Jakobson's pool house sits like an overfed silver marshmallow at the south end of her Long Island backyard. But for rabid fans of the Airstream aesthetic (including actors Sean Penn and John Travolta), the hand-riveted-aluminum trailer represents, as Jakobson puts it, "one of the key objects of 20th-century design." And she should know. A trustee of New York City's Museum of Modern Art and a serious collector of contemporary art and industrial design objects, Jakobson had no doubts about purchasing one of these funky mobile homes. "I had to annex an Airstream to me, as a person," she explains, "but I had no intention of going around in one." A weekday Manhattanite, she also faced the problem that confronts all collectors: where to put the thing. Near the pool, she says, "was the only logical place." So, eight years ago, Jakobson located a dealer in New Jersey who was selling a 1973 model aptly dubbed the Land Yacht. She had the 21-foot-long trailer hauled to the end of her pool with little hassle. No site preparation, no grading, no foundation—instant retro retreat. And while Jakobson did have to rip up the original orange shag carpeting after mice discovered it, she kept the gold-brocade upholstery on its two banquettes, which pull out to become a single and a double bed. In addition to housing guests in her Airstream, Jakobson serves drinks from its galley kitchen and escapes from the sun beneath its striped awning. These trailers may have gotten their name for the way they cruise down the road like "a stream of air," but Jakobson has no intention of moving hers an inch from the pool.

Melissa Davis writes a monthly Internet column for House Beautiful *and coauthors Carolyn Roehm's lifestyle books. Her work has appeared in* Vanity Fair *and the* Washington Post.

JOSHUA PAUL (2)

NOSTALGIA, FROM THE OUTSIDE IN: Jakobson's Airstream is reminiscent of the earliest models, which founder Wally Byam built in his L.A. backyard during the 1920s. At the end of the pool, opposite, her trailer is flanked by a white Vico Magistretti table and chairs, as well as custom cypress chaises shaded by a striped umbrella. Left: A view of the trailer's interior offers a glimpse of the galley kitchen and two banquettes. Though designed for travel, the durable walls—laminated in wear-resistant vinyl—come in handy poolside.

Contents

Introduction

The country was once a place of toil and production, a hard life of backbreaking labor. Only a few eccentrics—exiles and hermits, poets and philosophers, the ardent naturalist or pining lover—would chose country-living. With the Industrial Revolution, however, not only was a centuries-old way of life overturned, our notion of the country changed dramatically.

The massive rural exodus, the growth of the metropolis with its stress and pollution, the need to flee the jungle of the cities and the accompanying popularization of leisure, have instilled unsuspected virtues on rural life, shown country-living in a new and attractive light and revived the yearning for a paradise lost. For city people, the country represents nature as it should be; a simple, leisurely life and landscapes resplendent in their beautiful attire. Far from the maddening crowd, the city-dweller can indulge in childhood reverie, pay his debt to Mother Nature, put down roots and take up the natural rhythm of the sun and the changing seasons.

The country houses of our parents' generation were often old rural homes or at least closely inspired by them. A whole generation recycled the shells of farmhouses, rustic barns, sheds and stables, restoring the vestiges of a rural architecture on its way to extinction. And they did so with the best of bucolic intentions and a good dose of nostalgia for days gone by. But with their natural discomfort and exorbitant cost of upkeep, these homes, including Marie Antoinette's hamlet and ruins of a water-damaged estate, soon showed up the limitations of the "simple" life. Common sense, not (it turns out) the sole prerogative of country folk, did the rest.

Today we build not so much country houses as houses in the country. This is an important distinction. The only major difference between houses in the country and their urban or suburban counterparts is the size of the land they occupy (at an incomparable price) and their often breathtaking views over unspoiled landscapes.

This book covers a wide spectrum of houses throughout the Western world, from Europe to North America to far-off Australia. Designed by renowned contemporary architects, they illustrate by their diversity their common attachment to the particular character of a place and the challenge of integrating a human habitat within a natural setting.

Above all, these houses attest to the aims of those who live in them, their commissioners—the homeowners themselves—the realizations of their ambitions or ways of seeing the world... their dreams. While they put forth myriad visions, all belong to a single notion, the notion of happiness.

Sign of the times and record of the past, a showcase renovation of an 18th-century farm.

Charles Gwathmey, Robert Siegel and Associates

A House in East Hampton, United States

Well-situated on the edge of a lake, the estate is comprised of two distinct buildings. In this converted farm, the old stables make up the main house. A long and low pavilion contains a small studio, the technical facilities and the garage.

Opposite:
Rows of beautiful pear trees between the low pavilion of the entrance porch and the old stables, flanked by the round tower of what used to be a grain silo.

On Long Island's south shore, only three hours drive from Manhattan, the Hamptons are a true haven for affluent New Yorkers, including a number of celebrities in the entertainment business. An increasing number of the area's farming estates and rural homesteads are being converted into country houses.

Long Island has a long history behind it and its villages are some of America's oldest landmarks. When the delicate question arises of obtaining a building permit, local authorities tend to welcome proposals to restore the area's old barns and windmills; besides, farms and rural estates are not in short supply. Here, the architects Gwathmey and Siegel have transformed a cluster of buildings belonging to an 18th-century farm into a beautiful residence.

Robert Siegel and Charles Gwathmey have been partners since 1970, the latter well-known in New York architectural circles. By the late 1970s, he joined the group of "Five," bringing together Richard Meier, Peter Eisenman, Michael Graves and John Hejduk. Also known as the "Whites," they proclaim as their forefathers the European avant-gardes of the 1920s, most notably Le Corbusier. Their projects are characterized by predominantly white, pared down volumes, geometric

The original posts
and beams have been
preserved and kept
in place. The oak wood
parquet is new.

compositions that affirm a new modernity in strong opposition to the American post-modernist ethos of the "Grays," who draw their inspiration from Robert Venturi or Robert A.M. Stern. Gwathmey and Siegel have made a name for themselves with their extension of the Guggenheim Museum, the large ten-story tower alongside Frank Lloyd Wright's famous spiral.

The Spielberg residence is one of Gwathmey and Siegel's most mature works. Paradoxically, its "soft" modernity would appeal to the "Grays" with its respect for the setting and its use of traditional materials such as the wooden shingles on its wide slanting roofs. Beautifully situated on the grassy shore of a lake, the residence consists of more than one main building. The house proper comprises two main living rooms, separated by a strictly laid out pear orchard and a swimming pool facing the lake. To the east, a long and low pavilion forms a porch in the way of an entrance with a covered pathway, technical facilities and a small studio, followed by a garage and a long verandah where the pool begins. Further up and dominating the landscape is the reassuring presence of the old stable, flanked by a rounded tower, originally a grain silo.

What was once the barn has been converted into a vast double-height living room. Cured of its scoria, the old framework is an essential feature in the overall design. A remarkable double staircase rises up through the center between two pillars. The eye is drawn upwards to a skylight, following the beauty of the staircase's complex geometry, sculptural effects and rhythmic rise and fall of its balustrades. From east to west, it separates the entrance and utility rooms from the living room, clearly occupying the central axis of the house.

The living room is spacious and bright, with the possibility during the summer to open its tall window and drink in the countryside of the Hamptons. In winter, its round open fireplace, built into the base of the stairway, brings the room closer.

Throughout the central space, the two floors are supported by the old stalls of the stable. The upper rooms overlook the living room through often humorous indoor windows, complete with shutters. The south wing holds a guest room on its first level, a small relaxed sitting room and two separate bedrooms above. The north wing has a kitchen and dining areas on the ground floor and the owners' private quarters upstairs, nestled beneath the attic roof. In the same spirit as the living room, the main dining room shows up the

A double stairway
framed by four wooden
posts rises up between
the living room and the
entrance.

Ground floor plan.

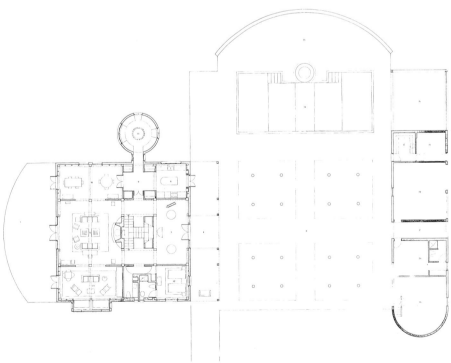

Wood alternates between old and modern:

oak wood parquet, beams

and floorboards from the old barn,

dark wood furniture and fixtures.

Opposite:

A center piece of the living room,

the large fireplace in a semicircle is

a favorite spot for family gatherings.

The master bedroom nestled under the sloping roof of what used to be the attic.

Opposite:
Once the stalls of the stable, the living room takes up the full height of the building and opens out generously to the landscape with its large picture windows.

stratification of the building's history, its different ages and types of wood—the contrast between the new light-colored oak floorboards and those from the old barn, or the sober dark wood furniture from the beginning of the century. Adjacent to the north wing, the round tower is where the family can gather to enjoy breakfast or simply take in the three vistas of the peaceful surroundings.

Unraveling the course of time, this country residence articulates a subtle blend of past and present, creating an altogether timeless quality, full of charm, serenity and a touch of the picturesque.

Ernst Beneder

A House in Blindenmarkt, Austria

The idea of having a country house, of being able to get away to that ideal, inaccessible hideaway is certainly appealing, but it often falls short in reality. It turns out you can only get there three or four times a year during vacations, or for some special occasion. The other solution of having one's "country" house not far from the city brings with it its own set of drawbacks: a nearby highway, a suburban development plan, railroads, and all that accompanies proximity with a city. The Huf House belongs to the latter case. Its owners are both doctors, a young Austrian couple who wanted a place to rest, to get away from the city.

The site slopes down to a small man-made lake bordered by trees. This just about sums up the dreamed-for change of scene. As for the rest, the house is pinched between the intersection of two roads. This is the "drawback" involved. The architect Ernst Beneder chose not to alter the site per se, preferring to ignore the unattractive element of the surroundings. Without screens or enclosures, he simply built two free-standing walls to the west side of the house, in the axis of the intersection of the roads. This sets up a symbolic boundary, as it were, and marks the beginning of a gravel path leading to the house. Apart from a few trees, nothing else comes between the lawn and the asphalt. In other words, the house can be seen from all around, especially from the north side where there is very little vegetation. On this side, the building literally turns its back to the road and offers only its shape of a parallelepiped, a "blind" facade that seems to have risen up from the soil itself. From this perspective, a passer-by is not likely to look any further. To reach the lake, one must cross the property, along the gravel path, across the stretch of lawn and alongside the house where a few steps lead down to its shore. This is the much-needed "miles away" feeling to the house, a spot hidden from onlookers. Here the building comes fully into view with only half of its length actually resting on the ground. Suddenly it takes off at the point where the ground slopes down to the lake and from its concrete base penetrates the empty space above the water. This weightlessness is all the more impressive considering its bulk and the few openings on its gray exterior—a large picture window overlooking the lake and the opening forming the entrance on the western facade. One enters the building on the side through an opening supported by a canopy-like structure crossing over the path. Turning left, you enter a small courtyard spread with gravel. To the right, the adjoining space opens out to the dining and living rooms, whose length forms a long view that culminates in the vanishing point of the window

Upon entering the property, two expanses of concrete wall form an enclosure without actually delimiting the terrain, but they do discourage curious passers-by.

Opposite:
The house is on the edge of a man-made lake in the Ybbs valley in southern Austria. A gravel path crosses a stretch of lawn, passes alongside the house and ends where a few steps lead down to the lake.

A small open-air courtyard
with a single tree forming
the entranceway.

facing the lake. The idea seems relatively simple and the layout straightforward; yet, can one really trust appearances? What appeared to be the entrance hall from the outside was in fact an open-air courtyard. Here a metallic staircase appears to lead nowhere; or perhaps we have forgotten to mention a roof terrace, or the private quarters of some nighttime haven? Beneder undoubtedly derives satisfaction from disturbing the perception of the observer. The only access to the bedroom and its bathroom is carefully hidden, and these rooms are set apart in the corrugated iron tower on the northern facade.

These are some of the ways Beneder tackles a difficult site. He chooses the view of the lake and projects the house forward to take full advantage of it, turning attention away from the other side. Finally, he focuses everything on the curious edifice itself, in some senses the only true point of departure.

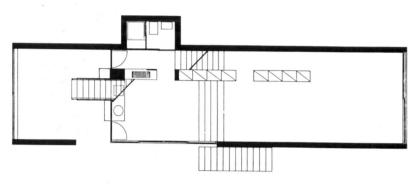

Ground floor plan.

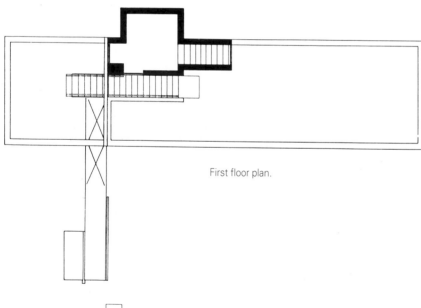

First floor plan.

Opposite:
The house seems to hang
precariously over the lake.
The cantilever is formed
by two slender iron posts.
Indoor life takes place
within a single space,
incorporating the entrance,
kitchen, fireplace, living
and dining room.

A metallic staircase leads
to the roof terrace from
the open-air courtyard.

Longitudinal cross-section.

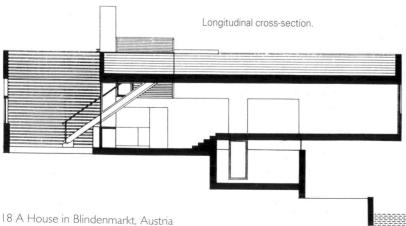

The reflection in the lake
accentuates the feeling
of weightlessness.

Opposite:
A square tower built into
the northern facade sets
itself apart with its
corrugated iron cladding.

While each area is articulated
by an interplay of different surfaces
and steps leading to the terrace
or the living room, activities take
place within one space,
occupying the entire parallelepiped
of the house.

Occasional fog obliterates the view
of suburban surroundings.

Opposite:
A peaceful haven, an inaccessible
hideaway... Nearby traffic of cars
headed for Vienna or Linz prove
this to be just an illusion...

Werner Hunziker

A House in Sempach, Switzerland

The town of Sempach, on the eastern shore of the Sempach Lake, was the site of one of Switzerland's most glorious battles. It is now an historic landmark. In trying to preserve this heritage, Sempach, like neighboring Lucerne, zealously guards the orthodoxy of its architectural landscape. It was not surprising then that this house with its glass and blue aluminum structure bruised local sensitivities.

A very precise dream is at the origin of this project. Long before it was built, the homeowner envisioned a house in the shape of a cube. The local community viewed the project as too eccentric, even as a provocation. It might never have seen the light had the architect Werner Hunziker not stepped in. Ever since he created his own firm in 1970, his bold projects had been controversial. Having as many detractors as admirers, he was thus honed to dealing with such situations. Tough negotiations with the local board lasted for two years before the project was finally accepted.

Beginning with the original idea of a cube, he eventually shifted the plan, forming a quadrilateral comprised of three identical squares. The third square is divided diagonally, the tips of the two halves removed and subdivided in two. These latter portions are then tacked onto the sides of the quadrilateral. While its initial surface remains unchanged, the resulting shape

An outside staircase rises up like a shield, protecting the facade from snow flurries and strong winds.

Opposite:
On the aluminum plated facades the nuts and galvanized jubilee clips are like an ornamental motif.

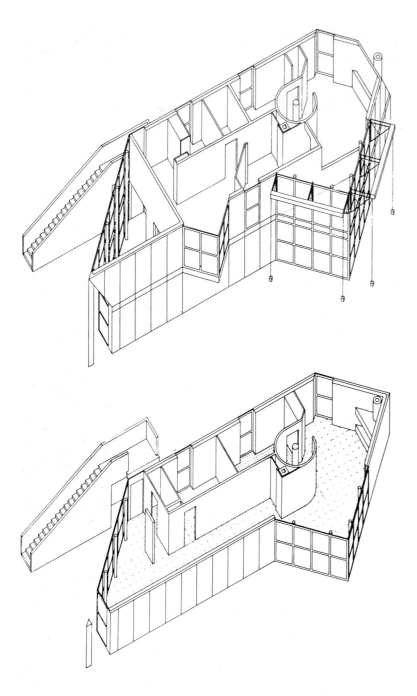

Axonometric plans of the house.

Opposite:
The protruding angle of the study in a complex geometrical volume: the "third square" is divided diagonally, the tips of the two halves removed and subdivided in two, these latter portions then tacked onto the two sides of the quadrilateral.

is clearly innovative. With its projected angles, the entire building seems to thrust forward, reaching out to meet the leafy forest.

This dialogue with the natural surroundings is the essential point of this design, which attempts to highlight the beauty of the environment while simultaneously protecting itself from it as the winters are particularly harsh in this region. The organization illustrates this aim. The living spaces spread out over two floors. On the ground floor, a double-height study surrounded by glass walls sits in the midst of the foliage and vegetation. But the outdoor staircase raised up on the side of the building like a shield, protects this side from snow flurries and icy winds. A library between the study and the living room provides a draft-proof, more enclosed area to retire to in contrast to the other, light-filled rooms with their large windows. The cozy corner around the fireplace near the living room also provides a refuge during the winter months. This area extends into the dining room, followed by the kitchen. The ground floor also has a guest room, while the other bedrooms are upstairs, along with the small independent quarters which can be reached from the outside staircase.

Werner Hunziker's talent lies in this double feat of conserving intimacy while allowing the occupants to enjoy the country surroundings and proving that country-living does not come at the expense of innovative design. His choice of materials illustrates his craft: repeated use of glass with steel framing, slate floors or simple white tiles for the kitchen and bathroom. His most striking feat is his bold use of a robust blue aluminum plating for the facades, its nuts and galvanized jubilee clips repeated throughout like an ornamental motif.

This blue house may evoke a mythical ship in an emerald sea for some, but the local community remains unconvinced. All the same, thanks to this design, the historical little town of Sempach may one day earn an honored place within the history of late 20th-century architecture.

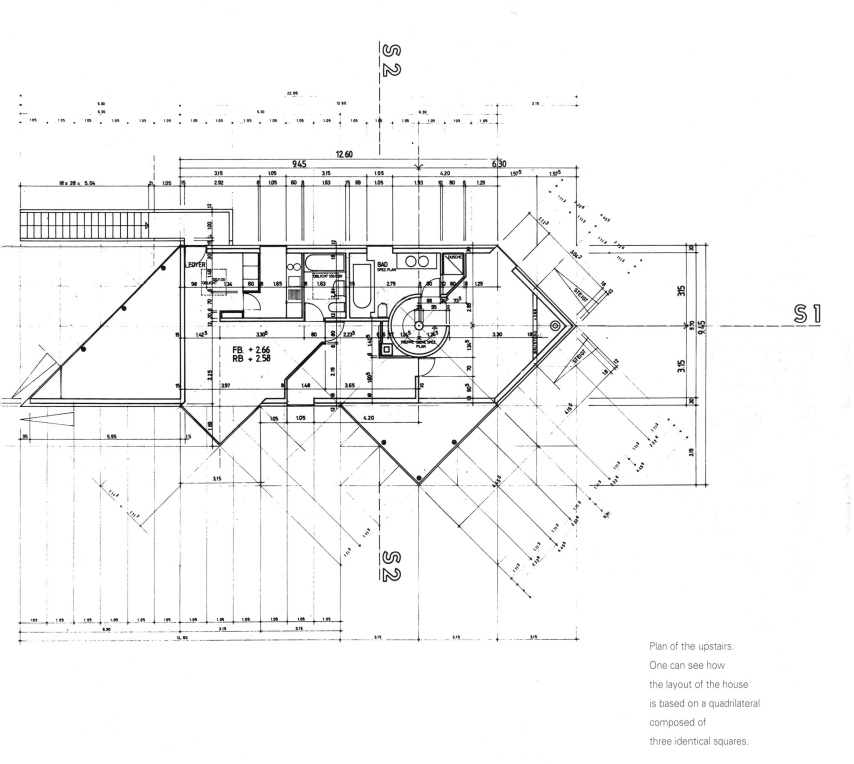

Plan of the upstairs.
One can see how
the layout of the house
is based on a quadrilateral
composed of
three identical squares.

Opposite:
The transparent facade,
with its framed glass
expanse, is a way of
absorbing the landscape.

The double-height study
on the ground floor takes
up the prow of the edifice.

Opposite:
The library, between
the study and the sitting
room, is draft-proof, with
no view of the outdoors.
It provides a retreat from
the other rooms with their
large windows.

A House in Brescia, Italy

The house is composed
of two distinct units:
the annex to the west
and the main building to
the south.

Opposite:

The main building is
typical of an elegant 19th-
century Lombardy home.
By adding openings on
the ground floor, the
architects have introduced
more light and air into its
main rooms.

In the late 19th century, this was a "true" country house tucked under a hill next to a village. Today, it is in the heart of the suburb of Brescia; although with its large grounds and provincial air, it still has the feeling of an enclave far from the city. Dilapidated, unlivable by today's standards, the house was commissioned to two architects, Ottorino Berselli and Cecilia Cassina, who specialize in renovating old buildings.

Enclosed by walls, the site is rectangular with two independent units, the annex to the west and the main building of the house proper to the south. The ensemble is surrounded by a large romantic-styled garden, lawns and groves of trees, and inspired, secret little nooks.

The main three-story house is typical of an elegant 19th-century Lombardy home. The architects first task lay in introducing more natural light into the ground floor where the large rooms were dark and airless. We tend to equate sunlight and open spaces with our enjoyment of life, wanting to appreciate our natural surroundings while staying indoors. In seeking to meet these aspirations, the architects punctured the walls with four large windows surrounding the central room where all the other rooms, except for the kitchen, converge. Another notable addition is the staircase that joins the floors without diminishing the space: an airy, linear flight of steps with the simple line

Built on a rectangular site at the foot
of a mountain—today a suburb of Brescia—
the house is surrounded by a romantic-
styled garden.

The large living room
with contemporary art
and chairs has preserved
the 19th-century charm
of a patrician home: marble
floors, light walls with
molding, mirror effects and
a large Venetian chandelier.

Detail of a metallic leg
of a glass table.

Opposite:
Old and modern side by
side in perfect harmony.

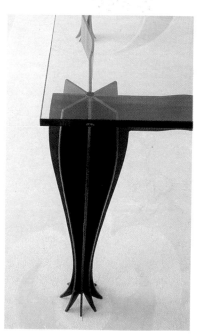

A succession of rooms
paved with two different
tones of marble and
strewn with a number of
contemporary sculptures.

Opposite:
The architects have left
areas of bare stone
"framed" by white
plaster or sometimes
plaster surfaces offset
or "framed" in stone.

of its metallic handrail. The original floors on the second level were polished, some of the walls taken away and the order of the rooms re-arranged. The bedroom and bathroom, for instance, were put side by side for practicality. Once again, the architects' aim was to increase the volume and bring in more natural light, taking advantage of the balconies and terraces. The last floor is a single room for multiple uses. It has extra beds, a bathroom and a large central space with an imposing brown overhanging structure supported in the middle by a thick pillar. As well as a place for storage, family and friends can gather together here in shared play and games, for those convivial activities that change according to circumstances and the seasons.

The annex is made up of an old part and an extension added in the 1960s that formed an odd ensemble. Here, the space needed more coherence and, hence, the architects created two distinct units on two levels. The first unit is an extension of the main house, providing extra utility rooms, and on its ground floor adding a large hall or dining room. Upstairs it holds a gymnasium, showers, changing rooms and a solarium. The second unit has become a guest house.

The principle was to keep the original style of the house without compromising comfort and volume. Thanks to the architects' innovative and discreet renovation, the facade has kept its original identity and character. The large living room, while significantly altered, conserves its 19th-century charm. Marble floors, light walls with molding, the use of mirrors, large Venetian chandeliers, along with contemporary furniture makes for a distinctive atmosphere, unassumingly elegant without losing its endearing touch of provincialism.

A House in Sonoma, United States

A monumental entrance
on the northern facade
with its two somewhat
ironic blue columns.
The glass door reveals
the elongated hallway
and the view beyond;
one enters the landscape
"outdoors." The two
main buildings are
connected by a portico
supported by blue
columns that describe
an offset symmetry.

The splendid Knipschild Residence was built in the 1980s at Glen Ellen in the heart of Sonoma Valley. Northern California has a mild climate and plentiful sunshine, to be enjoyed all the more from this house at the top of a hill with its stunning view over the famous Valley of the Moon where Jack London also dreamed of having a country house. His dream came true, or at least for a time. The "Wolf House," as it was known, was a costly undertaking; the day before its inauguration, the sumptuous yet ruinous abode went up in smoke.

The Knipschild Residence is now a proud addition to California's architectural patrimony. A subtle blend of styles and references, an allusion to the Mexican hacienda and a touch of 1930s glamour, above all, it is a rigorous contemporary interpretation. It won the Award for Excellence from the Sonoma League for Historic Preservation, a success owing to the work of architect Mark Mack from the Venice, California-based firm, Batey and Mack. Beyond his individual talent, however, the residence has the customary mark of Batey and Mack. Their approach consists of translating the client's needs into a plan based on a combination of rectangles, squares or crosses. These are assembled in turn to form the project's specific structure. The firm puts emphasis on communication at the early stages of the consultation. After toying with a rectangular-

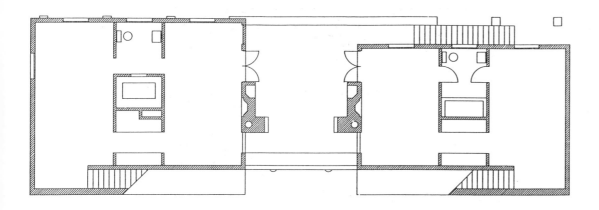

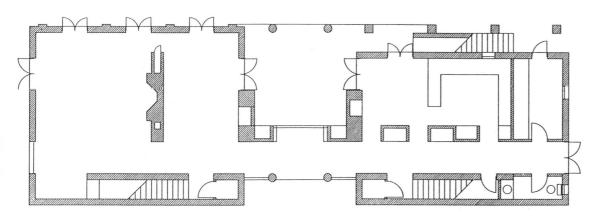

Floor plans: on the ground floor
two symmetrical staircases
integrated into the northern facade
lead to the terraces and bedrooms.
The central hallway provides
access to the two wings, a large
living room on one side
and a dining room and kitchen
on the other. The staircase
on the southern facade leads
to the owners' private quarters.

View of the northern facade,
its walls like wings of a butterfly
enclose the staircases leading
to the terraces.

Opposite:
The hallway extends into a patio
framed by columns overlooking
the pool and the valley below.

The owners' private terrace and
its steps. The exaggerated height
of the French windows with
their wooden frames set against
the ocher stucco walls.

shaped plan, the dialogue between client and architect gave birth to an H form. The result was a lively interplay of symmetry and contrasts, especially in terms of its two complementary facades: one side opens out to the bright sunshine and the valley, while the other is closed and compact. The south facade, in its delicate rosy hue, shared by the building as a whole, is exposed to direct sun and the stunning views. The two cubic and, apparently, separate volumes are connected on the exterior by a gray concrete portico, supported by its sky-blue columns, while indoors, one passes from one to the other along a transversal corridor. The ground floor rooms have French windows that increase the air flow and the penetration of light. This floor extends outside onto a terrace beside a pool. The turquoise surface of the water forms a transition between the architectural artifice and the natural setting.

In dramatic contrast to this openness, the north facade is resolutely closed, spreading out laterally like the wings of a butterfly. The main entrance, consisting of a glass door flanked by two blue columns, is its only opening. Through this door a wide reception hall in the center of the ground floor opens out to the living-dining room on one side, and the kitchen and utility rooms on the opposite end. Laid out on the same level, these rooms have easy access to the terrace and pool, and to the inspiring view of the valley below.

Each of the two volumes has an indoor staircase leading upstairs. A flight of steps built onto the south facade also provides access to the upper level where the owners have their private quarters, separated from the guest rooms by a small terrace.

The interior decoration is sober and classic, in the same soft tones as the rest of the building: ivory and slate-gray for warmth, gentle rose of the terra cotta to enchant the light, and a final note of turquoise, shared by the pool and the supporting columns on the facade. And last but not least, the glorious blue of the Californian sky.

The corridor connecting
the two wings with
the rhythmic design of
wooden beams overhead.
To the right, one
of the indoor staircases
integrated into
the northern facade.

Opposite:
The outdoor staircase
leading to the owners'
private terrace, marked
by a tall square post,
the concrete contrasting
with the red-ocher stucco
walls.

A solemn fireplace with its sober lines and brick
interior commands the spacious living room.
Its presence is tempered by opulent furniture.

Opposite:
The luminous corridor in terra cotta flagstones
with a rustic chest and a piano at the end, recalling
a Spanish hacienda.

Jo Crépain

A House in Gravenwesel, Belgium

In the heart of the forest,
a high rose-colored wall
in cement brick is
the backdrop, at night
and during the day, for
two symmetrical pavilions
on either end with their
œil-de-bœuf windows.
A classical layout around
a small courtyard with four
pillars, topped by vases
overflowing with wisteria.

Near the Gravenwesel forest, the refined outline of a villa, surrounded by three old beech trees, rises up in the middle of a clearing. A rigorous geometry dictates its volumes, and its overall planning illustrates an intentional orderliness, sobriety and symmetry. The De Wachters chose to have their home built in a residential area near Antwerp. The well-known architect Jo Crépain built his clients a true *Tempieto* (little temple) uncomplicated in appearance, yet sophisticated and refined in its references.

The organization of its volumes around a central patio alludes to ancient architecture; brick-colored breezeblocks, gray walls and light-colored slate roofs make reference to rural architecture; and its strict adherence to the rules of composition evoke classical architecture. The house's separation between daytime and nighttime space, between the quarters for the live-in help and the reception areas undoubtedly draws from a more modern concept of layout, taking its inspiration from the designs of American architect Louis Kahn.

A tall, long and narrow volume contains all the living areas. Called the "Wall" by the architect himself, it stands like a backdrop to a longitudinal stage, serving also to separate north and south, night and day areas. Punctuated on either side by evenly-spaced glass bricks, during the day, they let the natural

50 A House in Gravenwesel, Belgium

The entrance is the sole
opening on this otherwise
opaque northern facade.
A false colonnade
of square pillars and the
trompe-l'œil effect recall,
with a touch of irony,
a temple from antiquity.

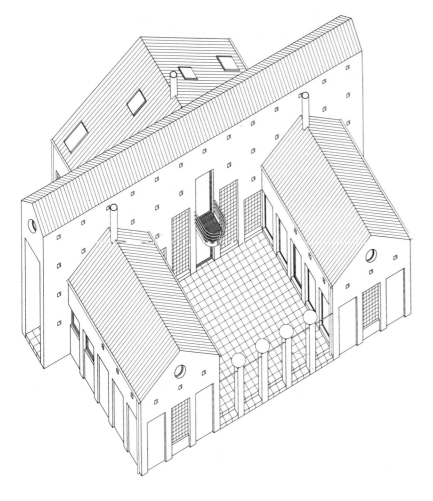

Axonometric plan: the "Night Temple" to the north, the "Day Temples" to the south opening out onto the small courtyard. The "Wall" in the middle provides access from one wing to the other.

Opposite:
Suspended awnings between the vase-topped pillars create a closed courtyard.

Seen from the northern facade's sunken entrance, the glass bricks have the same dimensions as the rose-colored concrete bricks.

light penetrate into the interior, while seen from the outside at night, they form a luminous squared framework.

Up against the north end of the building is the "Night Temple." On its ground floor and layered one above the other are the garage and utility rooms, with two bedrooms and their bathrooms upstairs. Its design forms the end piece with a *trompe-l'œil* portico, underscored by two tones of breeze blocks and its main door topped with an oculus, giving it the air of a home temple.

To the south, two symmetrical wings constitute the "Day Temples." Their large picture windows open out to a square courtyard surrounded by the living rooms. The ends of each "temple" are decorated with three *trompe-l'œil* porticos, a line of square glass bricks and an oculus. Four square pillars support basins overflowing with wisteria. These delimit the central patio and provide a transition between the house and the garden. Large screens can be rolled down between the colonnades to create a more intimate area. Cut into the backdrop of the "wall" is a monumental, almost Palladian-styled motif made up of a series of glass bricks which decrease in size and frame a high picture window. In the center of the "wall," a circular white metal balcony commands this distinctive atrium.

The villa is entered at the western end of the "wall." A double-height gallery allows for horizontal circulations. The staircase leading upstairs culminates the perspective. In counterpoint to the black marble floor on the ground floor, the upstairs has a metal grill that projects sharp shadows onto the white walls below.

To the west, the "Day Temple" closest to the entrance holds an open kitchen and dining room. Contemporary furniture and a bright red screen create a dynamic space. On the mezzanine is a room expressly for watching television. The east side, near the staircase, holds a spacious and bright double living room. Tucked underneath the duplex study is a black cast-iron stove.

To the north, under the cavity of the pitched roof of the "Night Temple," two symmetrical bedrooms, separated by their bathrooms, open up to the sky.

This villa brings together a clear organization of volumes, a subtle balance of forms, with the use of quality materials and varied lighting effects. The result is a convincing example of classical modern architecture.

The dining room, lit up
by its glass brick window
and oculus, is furnished
with modern chrome
chairs around a sanded
glass-topped table
supported by four chrome
posts.

Peter Lorenz

A House in Innsbruck, Austria

The Innsbruck-based architect Peter Lorenz opted for simplicity when he constructed the Miller House. After all, only modesty feels appropriate faced with such a grandiose site, its southern panorama of mountainous foothills, the Inn river and city of Innsbruck in the valley below. Instead of confronting this splendid environment, the architect chose to view the house as a pretext, or a permanent invitation, to enjoy the landscape.

The terrain, wooded with pines and broad leaf trees, is intact except for a walled-in trench rising gently up the slope, meeting the house at its northern facade, where it forms its base, then disappears into the garden before it ends in a terrace under the awning of a small portico. The main building is back to back with the axis of the trench, turning out deliberately to face the valley, but not without a little reserve and respect, seeming to take its cue from the environment itself.

The edifice is like a cube contained within an hermetic shell. It is closed on the northern side, the side that remains in the shadow and faces the cold winds. This initial structure evokes an inert, stony mass with its roughcast surfaces mixed with gravel and painted in hues of blue and gray. To the southwest, this cubic geode opens out suddenly, revealing what it contains and protects: the second structure. Developed over two levels, this second structure is lacquered uniformly in

The interplay of two cubic volumes, one inside the other, and set off at an angle of 20°, accentuated by their distinct treatment of materials: roughcast concrete against a facade clad in white wooden slats.

The shift between the opaque volume with
its mineral coating and the white volume
with its wooden slats forms a covered terrace
at the southwest angle of the house. This interplay
of two volumes sets up a striking contrast between
the mass of the outer "shell" and the dynamic
brightness of the inner white facade.

Opposite:
A little garden kiosk in the local Tyrol style
but adapted to modern tastes with its brightly
colored metallic structure fixed to a concrete base
and its taut curved roof.

white. Gray granite and snow-white, the Miller House stands like an homage to its mineral surroundings, but in no way losing itself thereby. Nothing could be more singular than the ingenious geometry of its two volumes fitting into one another. Its massive outer "shell" also sets up a striking contrast with the dynamic inner structure whose white facade is bathed in light and animated by vertical lines. This facade is streaked vertically by wooden slats that form the sides of the aligned windows of the verandah and the first floor. The verticals are further accentuated by two square pillars supporting the end projection of the "rocky" shell, overhanging the space and deployed like an awning. In a dynamic rendering of the ensemble, a small balcony from the bedrooms projects still further out, encircled by slender railings perched in turn on tall pillars. This colonnade effect is clearly a Palladian allusion and a marked characteristic of Lorenz's designs. The southwest facade is thus constructed to form the heart of the house, exposing the living room areas and private rooms to the sun and giving them a superb view over the valley.

The interior is resolutely sober throughout, but especially in the living room, where the kitchen and dining area converge. Here, the landscape seen through generous windows forms the main feature. The furnishings are kept at a minimum with no unnecessary flourishes. There are a few oriental carpets on the light oak floors and a fireplace, set with blue and gold ceramic tiles, with a closed-in fire—a contemporary version of the Tyrol stove.

Allusions to the local style are minimal and subtle. The open-air portico at the end of the trench recalls the small garden kiosks one finds in Tyrol. But Lorenz offers his own pared down, minimalist version. Yet, on closer examination, its turquoise glazing, its risers and the yellow-gold touch of its tension wires are not altogether devoid of affectation.

The Miller House's simplicity is clearly the end result of much in-depth and sophisticated research.

The bright, spacious interiors
are discreetly furnished: rugs
on the light-colored parquet
and the tall fireplace with a vertical
motif—a peaceful and comfortable
atmosphere.

Guillermo Vasquez Consuegra

A House in Mairena de Aljarafe, Spain

A theatrical air marked by an ambulatory around a cloister that disappears in dots into the landscape. The end facade, bare except for gaps in the guise of windows, is set off from the studio. The Casa Rolando sets a structure reminiscent of a De Chirico within the Andalusian countryside.

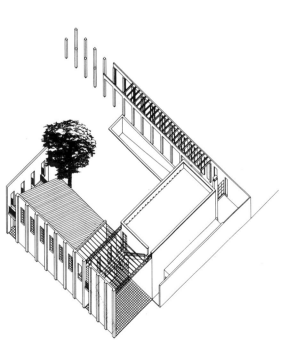

Built in the Seville countryside, the Casa Rolando is not a country house per se, although it lacks neither the charm nor the advantages. Its traditional structure recalls a hacienda, and like a true hacienda this is a place as much for work as for pleasure. A painter lives here, having moved in all his penates and his easel. The role of architect Guillermo Vazquez Consuegra was to develop several areas adapted to the painter's lifestyle and needs.

The house follows a square plan. Three wings meet at a straight angle, connected by a walkway that completes the geometry of the layout. Held between two lateral structures, the east wing develops over two levels, forming the main building of the house proper, topped by its roof-terrace. The kitchen, dining room and living room share the ground floor extending into a planted patio with orange trees where a verandah supports the advancing portion of the upstairs. Vanishing points are an important feature of the Casa Rolando, both for pleasure and necessity, as well as strong perspectives. Upstairs, the bedrooms take up two interior galleries. The largest one, lit up to the west and north by tall French windows, commands a view over the olive grove descending down the gentle slope of the Guadalquivir valley. To the south, it leads to

The main building on
two levels and the studio
with its pitched roof
articulate a space covered
by a metallic support
for wisteria to climb along.
What resembles an
arcade follows the length
of the facades to provide
shade from the intense
Andalusian sun.

Axonometric plan
of the complex.

Floor plan.

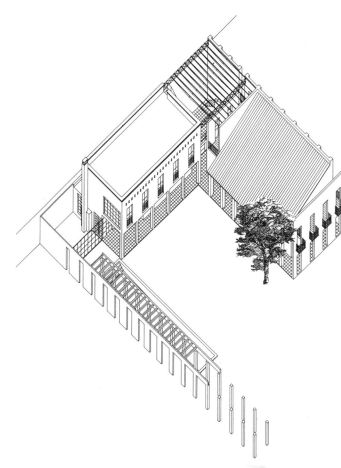

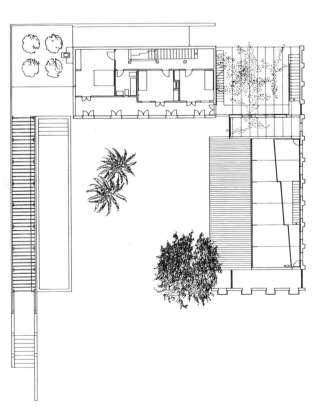

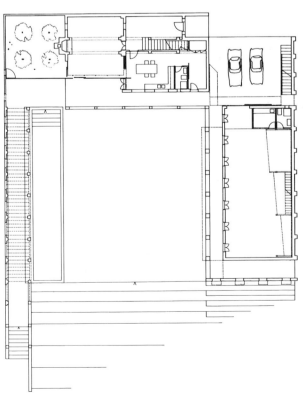

The space left free at the angle
of the two buildings is used for
parking. The metallic structure
above it will provide a support
for future climbing plants.

The two buildings are connected
on the first level by a raised metal
platform.

an atrium whose roof is intertwined with bougainvillea and other climbing plants, forming a pleasant extension of the living room areas and articulating a transition between home and studio. Of rural design, the studio with its large sloping roof of flat tiles, is a single spacious room, a neutral area with a green metallic structure overhanging the space. Daylight floods in through two strips of windows, one facing north in line with the floor, and the other set high up, accessible by a narrow mezzanine on thin metal posts. This gangway leads either back to the atrium or allows one to reach a series of small balconies built into empty window openings on a facade that appears to form merely part of the decor.

Distinctly different from the rest of the building, this facade stands out against the blue sky like the remains of an abandoned house lost in the Andalusian countryside. The architect happens to be Andalusian. The Casa Rolando is a testament to his deep attachment to his culture. The central plan makes a direct reference to the typology of the hacienda with its verandah on the facade for a rest in the cool air. It is said that the whiteness of the walls and the powdery blue window frames keep insects away—again an echo of tradition. The portico extending all the way to the olive grove takes the architecture to the fruitful soil from which it has drawn its roots.

The simple wooden staircase leads to the bedrooms upstairs. A raised metallic structure frees up the entire volume of the studio—no posts or other supports are necessary. From a raised platform along the northern facade one can enjoy views of the landscape. The bedrooms are organized along a corridor with large French windows that open out to a balcony.

Frank O. Gehry

A House in Wayzata, United States

Each room of the house has its own shape and corresponding materials: a truncated pyramid clad in black sheet metal, a slice of local stone, a parallelepiped in red Finnish wood, a shiny metal box perched up high.

Not far from Minneapolis stands a fine red-brick residence modeled after the patio houses by the great Mies van der Rohe, conceived of in his Berlin phase in the 1920s. It was built by the American architect Philip Johnson in the 1950s, at that time an ardent follower of the great European master.

The Wintons, who became its proud owners, have shown great respect for their home, which houses their collection of contemporary art. When the time came to build a guest house alongside it for their grown-up children and their families, the Wintons naturally called upon Philip Johnson. He declined the offer, perhaps simply too busy to take on another project or, which is more likely, having no desire to confront his past creation. He did, however, recommend Frank Gehry, being one of his earliest supporters.

Gehry is well aware of the eccentric nature of his designs and makes sure that his clients agree to the proposed plan beforehand. The collaboration with the client continues well into the construction.

The conception of the Wayzata House took many months to mature, with a number of trips back and forth between

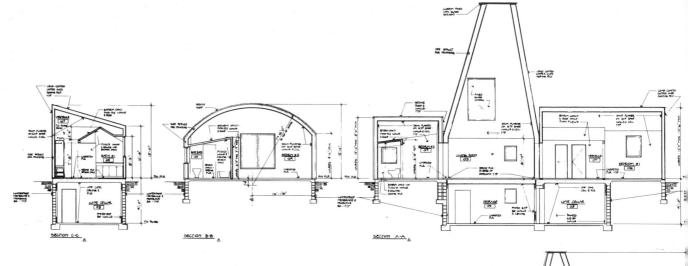

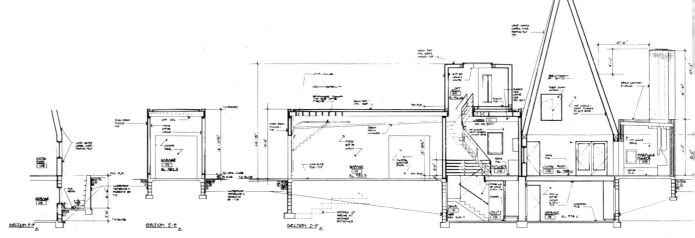

Cross-section and plan:
a centrifugal layout with
the living rooms in the
center, the bedrooms and
children's room (extending
from the garage) on the
outside in a configuration
suggesting a hamlet.

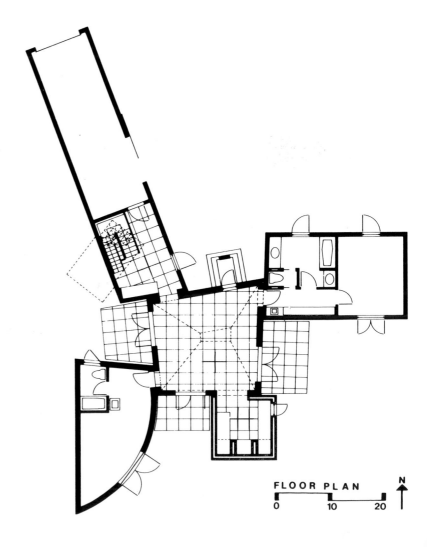

FLOOR PLAN

0   10   20

N

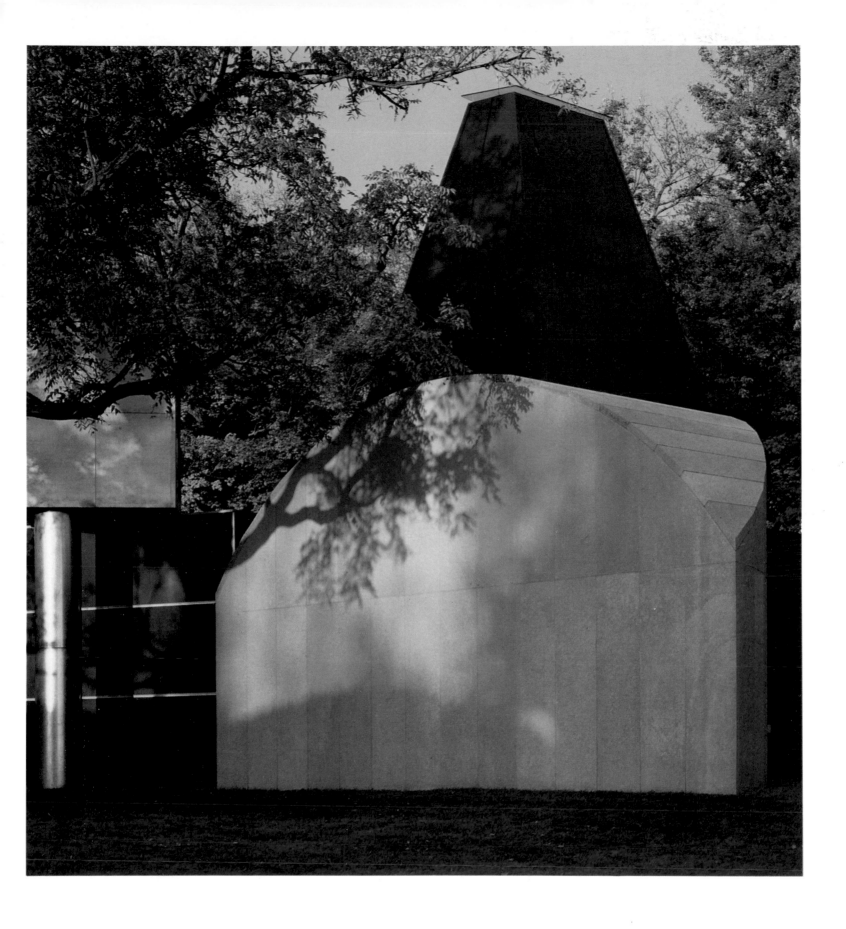

With the Wayzata House,
the architect evokes
Morandi or Chardin
still lifes with their
juxtaposition of assorted
objects making up a
sophisticated composition.

Los Angeles and Minneapolis. Its planning passed through many different phases; they even explored the idea of a pioneer log cabin but then opted for a less nostalgic project.

The Wayzata House reveals an idea that preoccupied Gehry at the time, that of a home as a hamlet or small village. His construction is thus made up of differentiated fragments that have been re-assembled—much like a Chardin or Morandi still life.

Nestled in the foliage, at a respectable distance from the main house, the guest house pavilion is a composite of six objects that are very different in shape, materials and color. A centrifugal layout articulates the "boxes" of shapes around a central truncated pyramid, clad in dark metal. This volume holds the living room. The parents' bedroom, shaped like a slice of cake, is faced with large kasota stone and local beige-colored stone. The kitchen and fireplace nook are held in a cube, topped by a square brick chimney like a red-brick oven. Two parallelepipeds lie on their sides, one housing the children's room and the other the garage branching off the central volume. One is clad in black sheet metal, the other in slats of dark-red Finnish wood. Finally, there is a shiny little metal box perched on a column, providing the children with their own secret viewpoint—a tree house, as it were.

Unlike the well-differentiated shapes of the exterior, the interior is fluid and light-colored throughout. Taking into account the harsh continental climate in this part of the country, the openings are kept to a minimum and their size carefully calibrated, giving each room its own particular framing of the landscape.

These two buildings, built at a 30-year interval, make this one of the rare sites where two periods in American architecture successfully merge.

Bart Prince

A House in Sun Valley, United States

It may be a great privilege to own a house built by Frank Lloyd Wright but when it comes to extending it with a new construction, the dilemma sets in, along with a guilty conscience. Who should one call upon? Does the master's spirit still live on in his disciples and guardians of the Taliesan West in Arizona? Henry Whiting naturally hesitated before he decided to deviate from the Wright dynasty, conferring his project to the extravagant Bruce Goff who worked in the central United States. But shortly afterwards, Bruce Goff passed away and the project was entrusted to his assistant, Bart Prince. Bart Prince had learned to tame his tutor's wild ways, to temper his teachings, leaving out altogether the totems and often incongruous materials of his master's rather endearing sins. Returning to a more organic style of architecture and often expressing himself through intentionally zoomorphic forms, he has derived a language of his own, a vocabulary well suited to the natural settings of his projects.

In Sun Valley (Idaho), Prince's plan incorporated the entire terrain allotted to him. Instead of defining a specific place, a supposedly ideal spot, he took it all, deploying his sinuous construction over the sand, choosing not to privilege certain views or create any hierarchy of perspectives. Built over two levels, the Whiting Residence blends into the surrounding hills and "looks" at the landscape from all its parts.

Two walls forming an S-shape delimit three distinct, semi-circular living areas, connected by a long corridor in the form

The outline of this low, undulating structure in the almost desert environment of Sun Valley evokes an antediluvian creature, a zoomorphic figure in the tradition of organic architecture.

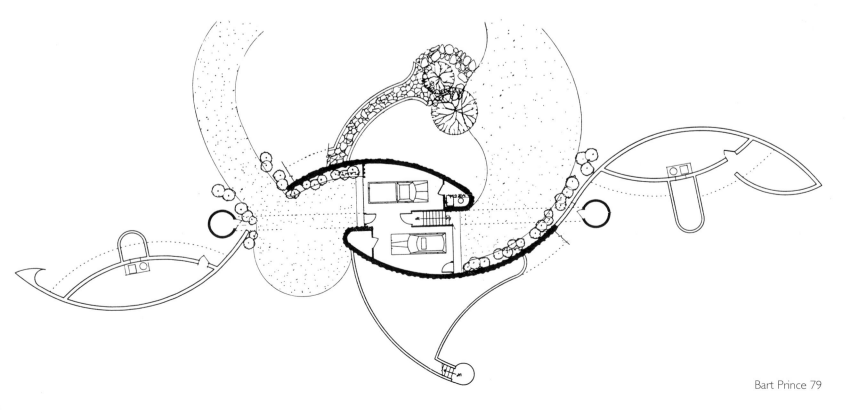

The bold combination of materials, the succession of curves and counter-curves spiked with sudden protuberances and unexpected breaks, the pointed windows—characteristics of an architecture that deliberately excludes right-angles, an architecture of the imagination and unbridled fantasy.

of a dorsal spine that forms an ally of light. It rolls out over a stunning framework whose ridge tile openings cast an array of spiked shadows as the sun's rays fall vertically through strips of glass, supported by a network of arched wooden beams. When the sun is at its zenith, it casts a geometric frieze of light and shadow along the entire length of the corridor's stone flagstones. At the center of the edifice, this axis of light sets off two spacious areas with the living room on one side and the kitchen and dining area on the other. At one end of the corridor, a ramp leads to the private quarters, with another ramp on the other end leading to the guest rooms and children's bedrooms. This sinuous, elongated layout makes for spectacular vistas—wherever you stand—through wide glass expanses along the length of its curved facades. Like a panoramic lookout post set in the heart of the desert, this surprising habitation is barely distinguishable, so effectively has the architect blended his construction into the environment. His use of materials illustrates this aim: the exterior is a mixture of glass and wooden tiles, echoing the ocher of the hills and the color of the sand. The interior is largely undressed stone and wood interspersed with white plaster and, here and there, small gray pebble gardens.

Exceptionally integrated into the surrounding desert, with its rich spaciousness and stunning views, the Whiting Residence illustrates Bart Prince's new path of what is proving to be an exciting career.

82 A House in Sun Valley, United States

The beast's belly is of smooth
wood, its back scaled
with an exquisite design of
shingles. Here and there,
a skylight or the amusing little
cylinder with its pointed hat.
A medieval spaceship?

Complexity of forms, the architect's free use of different structures, metal, laminated wood sidings, a stone bearing wall—a rare virtuosity. Bart Prince, in a tour de force, has landed an incongruous edifice in the desert that blends in perfectly with its surroundings... a paradox.

Lindsay Clare

A House in Buderim, Australia

Three discreet bungalows amid the lush vegetation with their clapboarding, corrugated iron roofs and large overhang. The house features all the characteristics of a burgeoning Australian architecture—astute, without a complex. The house follows a rectangular layout comprised of three distinct units: open living rooms and a more enclosed area and garage.

Buderim is a little town in the Sunshine West, a hundred or so miles north of Brisbane in the state of Queensland, Australia's Côte d'Azur. This is where the Goetz Residence covers a vast terrain of luxuriant giant ferns and enormous trees. Architecture's response to a tropical climate and intense sun must make use of experience and good old common sense. Straightforward tradition is the staple of local architect Lindsay Clare's design, without the weight of nostalgia or regionalism. Clare is far from a regional architect; each one of his projects responds to a very specific set of demands. Minimalist in its effect and means, the Goetz Residence project took into account a variable climate, the need for varying degrees of intimacy and the desire for a close relationship with its surrounding garden.

Following a rectangular design with three distinct yet connected units, the structure spreads out over one level. The living room areas—the first unit for relaxing and family life—have been carefully differentiated from the rest. On the North side, where the windows can afford to be larger under the roofs' awning, this unit is open and cooler. Behind its

An open space facing
north with its glass facade
shielded from the sun by
the large overhang
of the roof. A breeze-block
volume connects the two
units.

transparent expanse of glass, the area holds the living and dining rooms and the kitchen, all of which share an uninterrupted
view of the garden. The second unit on the south end of the
building is more solid and compact. Its closed, concrete walls
have a reassuring, sheltering effect for the three bedrooms and
library-study. A long corridor crosses between the two units,
thus linking the living room with this more enclosed area. Rather
than a passageway, however, this is a point of convergence
where all the rooms open out. The garage, the third and last
unit, is more firmly separated from the other two. The roofing
of large plates of corrugated iron set directly on top of the
wooden framework harmonizes this tripartite construction.

This use of untreated corrugated iron is a good illustration
of Clare's approach; he never looks with disdain at the local
materials, convinced from experience that they are most
suited to his needs. This is the honesty and seriousness
that so characterizes this architect. He also pays close attention to detail; the interiors attest to the importance he gives

to developing a rapport between colors and materials. In the living room, woodwork predominates, communicating its warmth of caramel-colored hardwood floors, varnished oak fixtures and the exposed light-colored and dark wood beams of the structure itself. The partition walls also function as screens, stopping two-thirds up from the floor to create a better air flow, providing imposts of light here and there. In the living and dining room, they are in white brick, while in the bedrooms they are concrete, their grooves painted green like the facades, an echo of the cool green surroundings.

The architect and his clients have agreed to let the project develop over time, a period that could extend over several years. By then the garden will improve and the spirit of the house take root. For Clare not only pays close attention to the passage of the sun and the direction of the wind, he listens to his clients needs. He collaborates with time itself, for the house to reach "maturity," before adding the finishing touches.

A synthesis of the colonial
bungalow with a Japanese
influence. The painted
clapboarded bungalows
are slightly raised off the
ground. A long corridor
unites the two units of
the living rooms on one
end and the bedrooms
on the other. The small
breezeblock volume sets
up a contrast with the
bright open areas and their
polished parquet floors.

Daytime and nighttime
areas have a direct rapport
with the natural
surroundings.
The simplicity of forms
and materials suggests a
simple and frugal life style.

A House near Gerona, Spain

A squat outline of a basilica, interspersed with palms trimmed like feather dusters. The *masia* has kept its original charm. An expanse of wall is punctuated by arched openings creating a theatrical air and outlining a pool, preceded by steps in local stone.

In Catalonia, the term *masia* is the generic name for a rural estate. With an architectural heritage that goes back to Ancient Rome, Catalan rural estates tend to imitate the form of a basilica, with their main facade facing south, away from the prevailing winds. Some are more assuming than others. They range from simple constructions built by farmers and small property owners to large estates of almost palace-like proportions. The house that has been renovated here by BDM, a firm in Barcelona, belongs to the second category. The residence is far inland, near Gerona, a good distance from the feverish excitement of the Costa Brava. The Empordà plains have prospered without tourism, and the Catalan intelligentsia continues to chose this area with its fine architecture to build their country houses.

This particular *casia* does not have an ideal locatation, however. At the bottom of a valley with no particularly interesting vistas, the only pleasant view is from the back side of the house. The architects chose to tacke this problem at the outset, adopting two complementary strategies. To improve the view, they added a number of attractive architectural elements: a large patio at the entrance, terraces, and a large wall pierced with two arches. On one side, the wall forms a protective semicircle around the pool, and on the other, it joins up with a

Open to the pool through two arches, the free-standing wall reveals a large shaded gallery and shields a flight of steps— a touch monumental— leading to the upper level.

metal portico, thus creating an open gallery. Not having any other choice than to work with the immediate surroundings, the architects took steps to make the property stand out. They planted a stretch of vines, and on the immediate grounds, small gardens and olive groves. Seen from afar, the now imposing estate attracts attention.

The original building has not been significantly altered. This house is a perfect illustration of the basilica style—mentioned above—with its numerous stunning elements such as the little watch tower or the barrel vault of the main living room. Naturally, some restoration was necessary, including the addition of some walls; but the overall aim was not to let the changes dominate. The architects simply attributed certain functions to each room, following the owners' wishes. The only significant alteration involved aligning the windows along the axis of the new disposition of the rooms and the outdoor arches. Some of the spaces lacked light, especially the large vaulted rooms, a problem the architects solved by replacing walls with glass of the same dimensions. The arrangement complete, only the finishing touches remained.

The electric lighting was studied in depth, aiming spot lights on beautiful features of the architecture or accentuating the arch of a ceiling and the lines of its supporting framework. The often freely interpreted use of color is also noteworthy: the interiors have either ivory, gentle ocher or yellow washes, giving them a touch of gaiety. Furnished with an odd assortment of objects brought back from various travels, some local, some ethnic, there are also very contemporary pieces. Nothing about the residence opposes this blending of old and modern. Beauty and necessity, the one with the other, add a natural quality to a well-balanced, remarkable ensemble.

Walls with traditional stonework, blinds with wooden slats shading the terrace and the outline of a little dovecote— all the rustic features are intact.

The beautiful vaulted
ceiling has been preserved
in the living room, but
the glass wall, with its fine
metalwork, has been
added, providing a full
view of the landscape.

Charming volume
of the beautiful attic
bedroom with its studied
lighting showing up the
arch of the ceiling. An
unusual blend of furniture:
the pillars of a copied
tester bed and skirted
seats give the home
a touch of humor
and the picturesque.

Gabriel Poole

A House in Noosaville, Australia

Noosaville, once a small fishing village on the edge of Lake Weyba, is a short drive from Brisbane, the capital of Queensland, in the north of Australia. This is where the architect Gabriel Poole chose to build his office and home. Poole has an eclectic background: he was a sailor at 17 and a foreman in the Queensland mountains before studying architecture at the Institute of Technology in Brisbane.

A fine connoisseur of the area, this spot near Lake Weyba had a special appeal for Poole. Half-hidden by the eucalyptus trees, two overlapping bungalows in metal, wood and glass stand out against the reach of a sandy terrain. From a distance, one could easily mistake them for traditional fishermen's huts. But their largely extended curved roofs, their gray wooden walls, their white-lacquered metallic structures, the glass latticework of pivoting screens and porthole windows evoke, instead, the shapes, colors and industrial materials used in boat building. A closer view reveals that this variety of forms, spaces, materials and construction techniques is a subtle response to the constraints of the site, to climate, orientation and the homeowners' own activities.

Gabriel Poole is an ardent admirer of Queensland's rural architecture, its light-weight constructions, the dark and cool kernel of the living space, the verandahs and the sloping roofs

Behind the relaxed appearance of this house with its assortment of materials—a do-it-yourself collage—lies great sophistication, the distinguishing mark of a generation of Australian architects on the rise.

These two buildings, one
for home and the other
for the architect's office,
match their natural
environment perfectly.
An achievement in its
economy of materials:
shiny corrugated iron
arched roofs with large
overhang, wooden
structures and walls.

Plan: the architect's office
to the left and the house
to the right with living
room, dining area and
kitchen. Clear section:
the upstairs bedrooms.

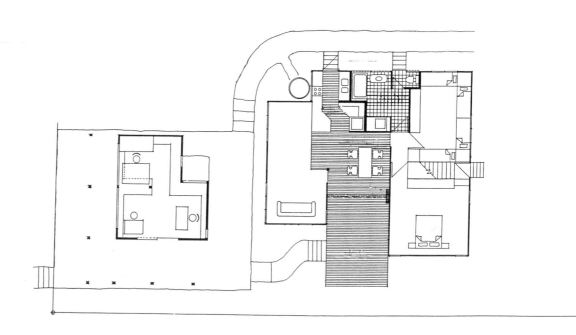

Cross-section: the house
proper raised off the
ground by short piles. To
the right, you can see the
staircase to the upstairs.

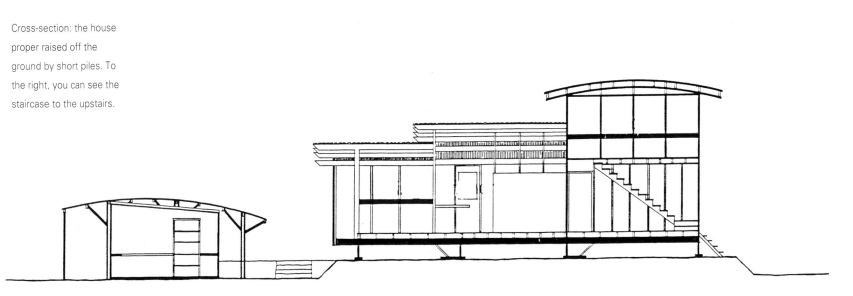

An almost rough simplicity of a wooden
structure with clapboarding, but offset
by the pivoting glass slats and the double-
layered roof of wooden slats, covered
by corrugated iron and curved metal tubing.

Following pages:
View of the interior with its hardwood
floors, square posts and plain wood beams.
The space is bathed in a diffused light,
reflected by layers of corrugated iron.
Furnishing of wooden tables, wood
and canvas chairs, Japanese paper
lampshades—a simplicity and comfort
chosen by the architect and his wife, painter
Elizabeth Pool. Her colorful paintings are
ever-present.

or awnings that shield the house from the intractable sun or the sub-tropical rains. Following in this vein, Poole has developed a rather more sophisticated and fragmented construction. Sitting on a bright red metallic platform, fixed to the ground with concrete piles, the volumes are broken up into two distinct parts. The two areas surround a fluid, elongated central space, containing the kitchen, dining area and a verandah, extended by an open terrace. Upstairs, the bedrooms, their bathrooms and a painting studio for Elizabeth Poole share the main building. Under one large sweep of the roof, a separate wing forms an extension of the central part, fanning out to a large living room. Further down, the study, like a dark box, is accentuated by the white daring curves of its exterior metallic framework.

Delicate in their design and application, a group of structural elements, double skins, projections, shifts, screens and roof extensions or awnings are superimposed—not without a certain amount of humor—over these initial layers. They give the house its dynamism and shield the interiors by capturing the breezes to increase the air flow, or simply frame different views, a piece of sky here, a section of landscape there.

The living quarters are almost entirely free of enclosures. Punctuated by the framework's thin white beams, they open out generously under their wood and metal ceilings. The oblique light gives the vaulted, corrugated iron ceiling its iridescence; in other places, light diffused by large screens of pivoting glass strips creates a variety of shadow, chiaroscuro, or all-over clarity. The blond wood parquet stretching the length and width of the central space gives way to areas with more cozy, gray carpeting. A relaxed atmosphere, simply furnished, the space vibrates with the many colors of an important art collection.

Gabriel Poole's house is another testimony to the emergence of an original Australian architecture, well-adapted to its natural environment and to the spirit of our times.

Nick Campbell, Roger Zogolovitch, Rex Wilkinson and Piers Gough

A House in Hertfordshire, England

A too perfect symmetry, studied harmony between roofing tiles and bricks, a pompous gateway with an urn on either side and semicircular fence, a rotunda entrance with white columns and an arched window above. One enters Howe Green Manor a little circumspect, like entering the world of Lewis Carroll.

A stately manor lost in the English countryside, such are bucolic dreams made of. But as the London architect from the CZWG firm Piers Gough likes to say, "It can be a lot worse than living in the suburbs." Gough was commissioned to transform a manor house in Hertfordshire, a county north of London, into an aristocratic home. The result is Howe Green Manor, a transformation that has avoided falling into the trap of becoming a conventional property and losing all the advantages of a country house, especially considering the notorious British climate. Gough saw his role as that of "helping someone in danger," and with this thinking let himself give free rein to his fanciful repertory, while conserving, at least in appearance, the local style. Self-proclaimed as having an eclectic style, Gough admits to a penchant for neo-classicism.

He has built a well-proportioned manor, following a square plan. One enters on the north side where, at the end of a driveway, an enclosed courtyard opens out to the main entrance. Two lateral wings frame a central two-story building adorned with a semicircular portico whose roof forms a balcony, followed by the arched window of the guest room. The main entrance is thus well in the bounds of a typical patrician entranceway. On either side of this facade, the walls

The other side of the picture is worth
the front: a round pavilion with hexagonal
roof and an orangerie with slanted walls,
topped with a cylindrical shape
and an *œil-de-bœuf* with the yin
and yang symbol.

extend and curve around, forming Chinese-styled pagodas, then reconnecting with the roofs of the lateral wings. This movement repeats itself on the south facade, maintaining a coherent layout of the roofs, their carefully chosen tiles, with the red-brick walls.

The interior is organized around an octagonal hall in the main entrance. Here, four doors at an angle lead to the main rooms on the ground floor: the salon and living room overlooking the garden, the billiard room and the study facing the inner courtyard. A corridor adjoining the study leads to the east wing where a long dining room is followed by the kitchen, which provides access to a breakfast salon, a back kitchen, a music room and the quarters for the live-in help, all of which are laid out in *enfilade*. Another corridor leads to the indoor swimming pool, one of the most impressive rooms of the house. Under its overhanging framework of small beams, the midnight-blue enamel pool reflects the repeated freize of the windows that light up this semicircular room. From here one joins the sauna and the gymnasium, which leads to the orangerie and then the garage opening out to the forecourt.

All the bedrooms are upstairs, reached by a wooden staircase at the end of the entrance hall. Light streams down the length of the staircase through a neo-gothic window above the landing, in the center of the south facade. From upstairs a gallery crosses the west wing and continues above the pool where two flights of steps form spirals, one of which leads directly into the water. The gallery also opens out onto the children's bedroom above the orangerie, then moves on to the private quarters, which have an individual entrance from the courtyard. Clearly, this residence has catered to its owner's every wish. A rigorous plan that lacks neither dignity nor comfort, and even less a sense of practicality; yet there are also an abundance of extravagant allusions and winks: the mischievous steps hovering above the pool, the assortment of windows—arched, gothic, French style, English style—a joyous assortment aimed at catching those rare instances of sunshine. Then there is the *œil-de-bœuf* with its philosophical yin and yang, and the curious design of the orangerie with inclined walls that recall an improvised military encampment. Neo-classical, fantastical... a parody. The Howe Green Manor is a history lesson in English architecture, complete with the signature-style of English humor.

An indoor swimming pool
and two high-tech (archaic)
stairwells like pulpits
and the reflection of the
windows that open out to
the garden—a decor
that would appeal
to the filmmaker Peter
Greenaway.
A double flight of stairs
with spiraled wooden
railings and, above,
a Victorian chandelier.

The orangerie has draped curtains,
reminiscent of the victorious general's tent
at Waterloo.

Opposite:
The ceilings decorated with plants
(poisonous?) and stars, the yin-yang symbol
framing a weeping willow in the distance.
This is the children's room...

Claudio Silvestrin

A House in Majorca, Spain

Behind the entrance
gap, the patio held
between tall ocher walls
with its white stone
bench—a deliberately
stoic aesthetic.

The house rises up like
a bastion between olive
groves and the Balearic
sky.

Before mass tourism laid siege to their coastlines, the Balearic Islands offered rugged and beautiful landscapes for a peaceful vacation. George Sand and Frédéric Chopin once consummated their romance here. The Mediterranean climate is ideal, with its refreshing sea breezes.

When Hans Neuendorf decided to build a country house in the middle of an olive grove on the island of Majorca, it was only natural that he turn to the architect Claudio Silvestrin. The two know each other well: Neuendorf, who has a well-known art gallery in Frankfurt, more than once requested the services of then partners Silvestrin and British architect John Pawson. Sharing the same tastes in contemporary art and holding the same reserves about vernacular architecture now very popular on the island but too often veering toward pastiche it made sense to opt for a resolutely modern house.

What Silvestrin proposed was bold and simple. The house with its massive volume and severe, minimalist style, has more in common with a monastery or a military compound than with an elegant home. An ocher outline rising up out of the olive trees, it shares the same earth-red colors of the vegetation and the soil, standing out dramatically against the Balearic blue sky. A graded paved stone path, shaded by

A covered patio at
the entrance to the pool.
The wide horizontal facade
is punctuated by only
a few loopholes.

Leading up to the
entrance, the steps are
shaded by a long wall.
The entrance is formed
by a narrow gap in the
facade, blind except for
one small loophole.

Ground plan: a square
and compact building
extending into the
landscape by its long
pathway along a wall,
by the pool and a tennis
court.

a long wall, leads gradually up to a modest, if not secret, entrance—a narrow gap in the concrete wall. Once inside, a large patio squeezed between the rampart and the main building provides a transition to the vast space constituting the only room on the main level. Behind the house, another patio, covered this time, overlooks a long swimming pool, seemingly floating in suspension over the neighboring terrain. Upstairs, the bedrooms are practically deprived of any view whatsoever, except for the children's rooms with their narrow loopholes, and one long and narrow window that lets in meager light. And yet light is the main theme of the house. Silvestrin has thoroughly absorbed what Barragan and Louis Kahn had to teach; he also draws from sacred architecture and such obscure sources as Ronchamp by Le Corbusier. Light enters sparingly through holes and thin gaps, for the most part from above, brushing across the pale coated surfaces of walls, showing up their texture, creating the effect of chiaroscuro or making the line of a wall shimmer for an instant. With this light play, the house gains depth and mystery and a mood of contemplation and serenity prevails. The floors of porous dressed stone from a nearby quarry muffle the noise of footsteps and give them a mat resonance in the empty spaces where furniture is kept at a minimum—a chair here, a sturdy table there.

Far from the futile bustle of holiday-makers, the house offers a well-disposed atmosphere for meditation, one that encourages reflection in surroundings where nature is plain and unspoiled.

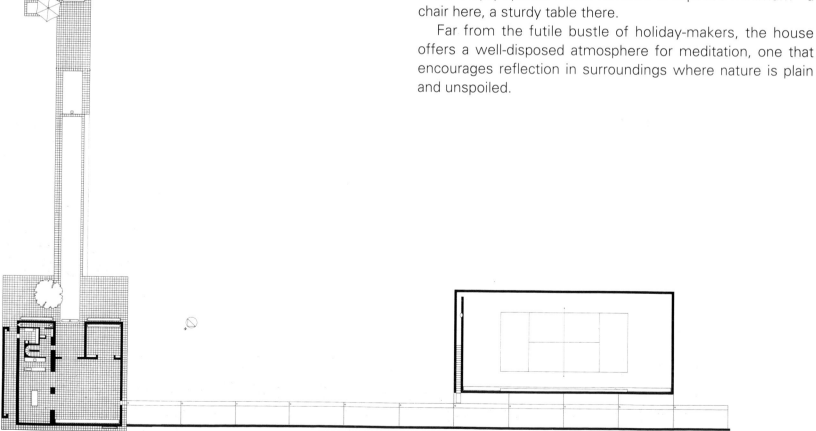

The swimming pool
is suspended above the
landscape. Another
smaller one below, filled
through a narrow passage
at the far end of the larger
pool.

The covered patio
provides access to the
pool and larger open-air
patio.

The entrance gap, the patio and the single vast room on the main level. The furnishing is more monastic than domestic: a stone table and a few chairs.

The master bedroom with light streaming in from above, brushing the walls in a play of lines of light and shadow.

A House in Wiesbaden, Germany

In 1989, the Z.B. Gallery in Frankfurt launched an architectural competition called "Aktion Poliphile." This was not the code name for some covert operation but a direct reference to the hero of the 15th-century allegorical romance, *Hypnerotomachia Poliphili*, whose esoteric adventure, with its mythical twists, is strewn with ruins, palaces and ancient temples. The Z.B. Gallery essentially chose this romance as a source of inspiration for formulating a thematic house. The prize went to the young British-Icelandic couple Margrèt Haroardottit and Steve Christer of Studio Granda.

Competitions of this type, especially those that tend to be high-brow, rarely see the light of day. In an exception to the rule, however, the Aktion Poliphile house was built, not far from Wiesbaden, on a site bordered by a huge expanse of forest.

The Studio Granda project comprises two buildings, a House of Saturn and a House of Delia, two figures who are related in the architect's tale, in an allegory well-suited to the conceptual framework of the competition. They constitute two visibly complementary designs: the masculine Saturn— a major figure in mythology often associated with Kronos, the relentless god of time who creates and then destroys his creation and the gracious Delia, the evanescent image of youth and modernity. The two distinct houses are joined by a raised passageway. The House of Saturn is solid and compact with its lead roofing and dark-red facades. One cannot enter its "blind," unadorned facade save where a simple curved wall like an indentation on the side of the building shields the entrance. This is the work space, the site of social relations. On its first level is a vaulted office and above, the private quarters and guest rooms. In opposition, at the other end of the passageway, the House of Delia designates an intimate space with rooms for day to day living. It advances toward Saturn from the forest, clad in the woodland dress of its beautiful cedar facades whose slats are set horizontally, forming a uniform structure. Thin beams in the same wood are superimposed vertically from top to bottom. The effect is spectacular, especially on the north facade where the vertical lines stop half-way down and jut forward like an horizontal herse. This wooden structure imprisons a roof garden that takes up the entire surface of the roof terrace. From this secret refuge, one can overlook the expanse of forest below. From here one can return indoors where three levels hold: the bedrooms and a living room lit up by the double-height picture window; the ground floor with the kitchen and dining area; the basement with a

Mythology as a pretext for building a house based on the theme of Saturn, merciless time, and Delia, fragile youth, beautifully illustrated by the British-Icelandic couple from Studio Granda.

garage and laundry room, and in its lower depths, a hedonistic retreat...

This Saturn-Delia couple create the strange polarity of this dwelling which constitutes, according to its architects, "an autonomous and private planetary system."

The House of Saturn:
an enclosed and opaque
lair for a timeless and
violent archetype. The
House of Delia: light,
blond lattice-work of the
facade and an awning
suspended by thin cables.
With its roof garden, the
House of Delia floats
above the wooded hills.

The dark tiles of the stairs
leading to the first level
in the House of Delia.
Its railing is made up of
"a tube from a tube from
a tube..." curving around
the cut-off end of a metal
beam.

Plan of the House of Delia:
the floor with its living
rooms and bedrooms.

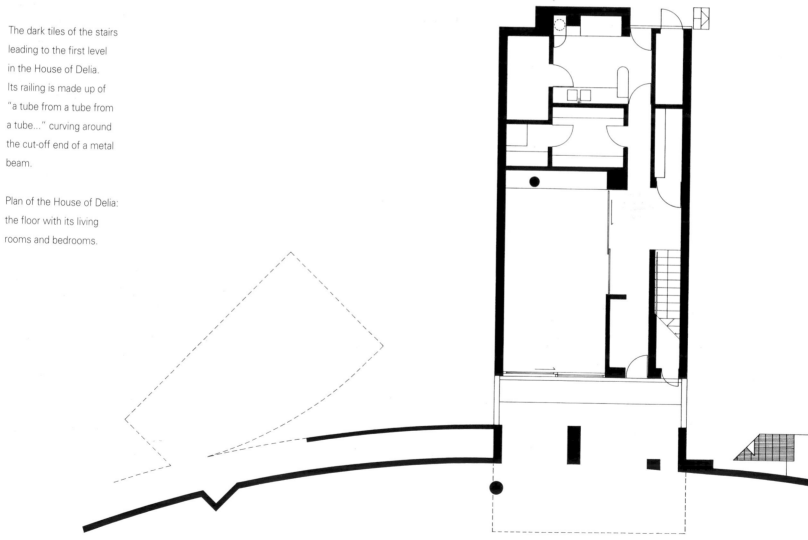

The implacable and cold
kitchen equipment.

Opposite:
Parquet floors and
wooden beams
on the ceiling frame the
otherwise shiny metallic
environment of the
kitchen and dining area
that opens out to the
landscape.

A House in Franz Valley, United States

A Californian ranch with Hispanic origins, its two verandahs, one above the other, a house perfectly integrated with its surroundings of wooded hills. An idyllic image of Northern California before the Gold Rush.

The sound of a rocking chair creaking back and forth on a wooden verandah—the stereotype of the American West. The image stems from folklore, from the pioneering age, an image that tends to blur with that of the rancher, after a hard day's work, resting in the shade. So much for nostalgia... This re-interpretation of the ranch—revisited in its most elemental form but surrounded, nevertheless, by the famous verandah—is clearly a going back to roots. The tradition itself of a covered gallery is not American in origin; it goes back to its early uses in Spanish architecture. Whatever the case may be, this house in Franz Valley with its splendid view of prairie lands and rolling hills, is an archetypical Northern Californian ranch, built with red cedar slats. The idea was put in the hands of the San Francisco-based architects Turnbull Associates, whose founder, William Turnbull, was a firm advocate of vernacular architecture and of showing the utmost respect for the site. His motto: "Keep the spirit of the place." One doesn't order the landscape, he would insist, one works with it or better yet, one integrates nature into the architectural project. This is the principle behind this residence built in among the trees, tucked into the heart of a grove of oaks. This decision was the response to a real problem and not merely an aesthetic concern—summer temperatures can rise to startling levels

The verandah and its
wooden balcony painted
white, standing
out against the red cedar
facade.

A shaded area punctuated
by its white posts,
the verandah is a place
for contemplation
and evening conversation.

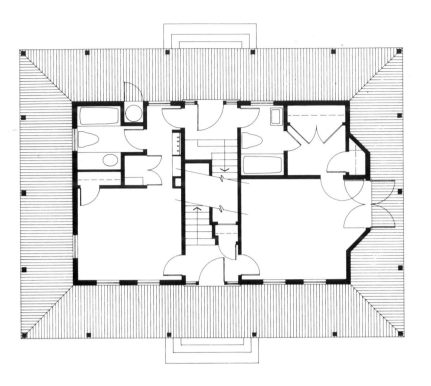

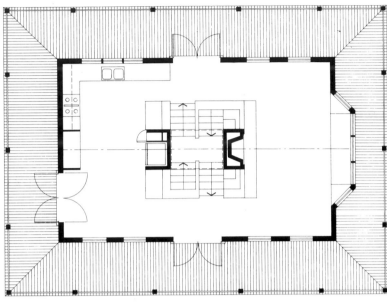

The architects have reversed the traditional layout of putting the bedrooms and bathrooms upstairs. Here, the upstairs is reserved for the living rooms.

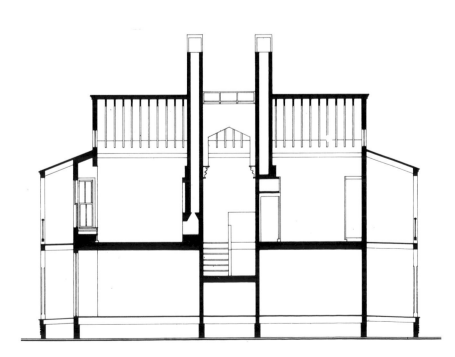

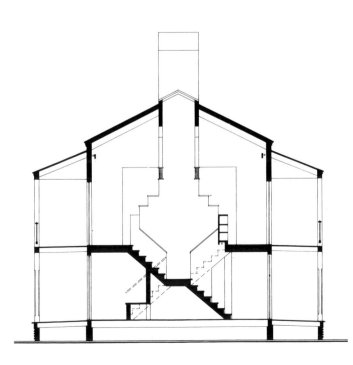

138 A House in Franz Valley, United States

in this region and every source of shade is precious. Thus, the wooden verandah encircling the ground floor and the upstairs is an effort to increase the air flow and filter the sunlight. Interestingly, this double gallery is also this large rectangular building's only decorative feature. White, gracious balustrades stand out against red cedar walls, adding a lightness to the ensemble—in a sense, a refreshing touch.

Indirect and very diffused sunlight comes in through the windows at an angle, while a central indoor staircase sheds perpendicular light. This vertical axis, built between the two chimney stacks, has a skylight perched high up, jutting out over the small pitched roof that supports the main roofing and adds extra height to the upstairs rooms. All the rooms are organized in relation to this source of light. The ground floor is unusual in that it groups together the bedrooms, with the family quarters separated from the guest rooms. In this way, the master bedroom opens out directly to where the prairie leads to the pool whose soft sound of flowing water comes from a small waterfall at its source. Upstairs, the staircase separates the kitchen and dining area from the living room. This upper level is cooler, having a greater air flow. It has a rustic comfort with country furnishings, exposed beams, oak floors and a fireplace. Everything in this country house keeps the bucolic dream alive. Complete with a back-to-the-earth fantasy, including a certain degree of comfort and luxury, it is every city dweller's fantasy for that future, "One day..."

A monumental staircase
in a central position, lit up
by a skylight between
the ridge poles of the roof.

The conventional kitchen,
dining area and the living
room organized around
the fireplace stem more
from the comfort
of city living than a rustic
simplicity.

D. Schnebli, T. Ammann, S. Ruchat-Roncati and S. Menz

A House near Zurich, Switzerland

The Miller House combines references to classical architecture with modernity: a cubic volume of sober gray cement bricks, crowned by a frieze and cornice; an alternation of tall or wide windows, and a rotunda entrance in glass brick.

After an initial period working in France and the United States, the Swiss architect Dolf Schnebli returned to his native country and settled in Agno, in the Tessin. This was during the *Tendenza* movement inspired by the late Aldo Rossi, a movement that viewed itself as an escape from the chimera of modernity, a rediscovery of architecture's natural laws and an effort to rehabilitate the "eternal" archetypes governing composition; but, as its motto claimed, with a "certain degree" of autonomy. In the late 1960s the *Tendenza* had taken root in the rather closed society of Tessin, its main players being the now famous Mario Botta, Luigi Snozzi, Aurelio Galfetti and Florat Rucha. Schnebli bore their influence, as the Meyer Villa suggests with its Palladian air and references to classical architecture.

Built in a natural clearing not far from Zurich, the site overlooks the distant shores of lakes—a true Arcadia in which the building itself puts the accent on serenity. Simple, pared down volumes conform to the spirit of the construction: a framework of nine squares at the base of three levels. An outer wall curves around the site, like an old-style border, hiding the entrance to the basement garage and utility rooms. Across the lawn and terrace, a large semicircular glass verandah constitutes the main entrance and adds

On the roof terrace
bordered by a cornice, a
small shiny structure with
a pitched glass roof
contains the elevator
machinery.

roundness to the rectilinear facades. It acts as a portico whose vertical framework is suggestive of a colonnade and does in fact function as one, adorning, as a classical temple would, the sacred threshold of the dwelling. It also lets an abundance of light penetrate into the hall that leads directly to a staircase with an integrated glass elevator. All the ground floor rooms are distributed around this central point: to the left, a kitchen, dining room, and a vast living room taking up half of the building's length, and to the right a work office. The bedrooms and bathrooms are all upstairs. The upper level has a roof terrace designed as a functional space. A roof garden hides behind the raised sections of the outer walls with their elegant openings that crown the building. A wide cornice tops the enclosure and forms a protective screen, preserving the brick facades and projecting over the perimeter of the terrace, giving it an open-air ambulatory quality.

Here, the elements that relate to classical architecture have provided practical solutions while adding their charm to the overall design. This, combined with Swiss precision, leaves not a trace of any excessive constraints. The living rooms are

Above:
The metal staircase
and glass elevator shaft.

Below:
The rotunda entrance filled
with natural light.

House plan: on the ground
floor, the entrance,
dining room, kitchen
and large living room;
study and sitting rooms
on the first level;
bedrooms on the second
level.

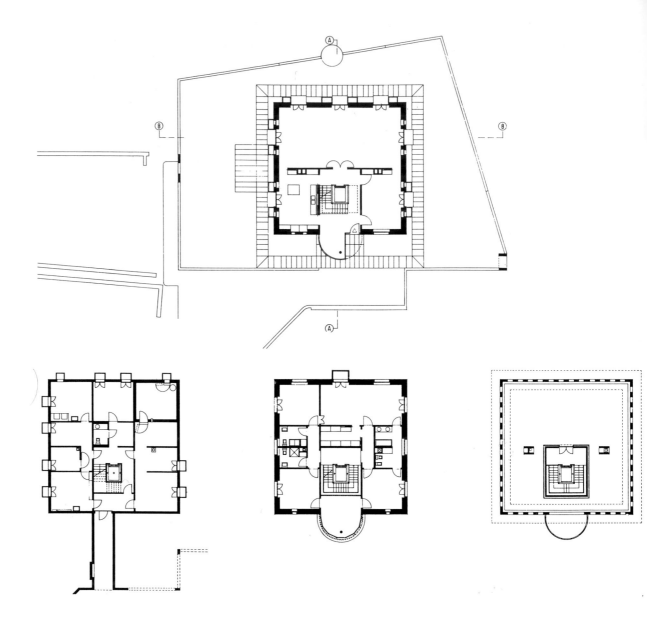

completely devoid of anything that might inhibit the eye or the sensibilities. Schnebli has favored total transparency: the glass verandah, the staircase whose steps, rails and elevator are in glass. In the same spirit, he has devised the rooms without contrivances to be large and almost empty, bright and smooth, with marble floored and with just a glaze of white plaster on the walls. One could almost say he is making an apology for emptiness as the place of freedom.

The layout takes into
account the vertical
circulation from
the elevator and staircase.
The landing with a Frank
Stella lithograph.

View of the large living
room open to the garden.
Here, a collection of
contemporary art includes
a large sculpture by Frank
Stella on the wall,
 standing sculptures
on the marble floor, a blue
and red chair by Rietveld
and chrome chairs by
Mies van der Rohe around
the table.

Richard Meier

A House in Harding, United States

The entrance is preceded
by an arcade joining
the separate wing—the
garage—with the main
house.

The cylindrical structure
holds the double-height
living room. The facade
is a variation on the theme
of the square.
The chimney, detached
from the facade, is like
a singular object.

Ever since he began in the 1960s, American architect
Richard Meier has had a consistent career. Alongside his
large-scale museum and public projects, he continues to
design distinctive private homes with growing mastery. He
was on the last stages of the J. Paul Getty Foundation in Los
Angeles—one of our late 20th century's most important
projects—when he started this country house in New Jersey.
It was initially commissioned by a close friend of the architect's. When the Grottas became its owners, they were
already familiar with Meier's style, his signature all-white villas
in the spirit of early modern architecture, and his principle of
working from inside out, repeating the layout of the rooms in
the openings. Meier is the master of compositions that are
balanced yet off-balanced at the same time. He views his
work as a continuation of a well-established tradition, claiming
that the subject of architecture is architecture itself. His center
of interest revolves around space, form, light and ways of
creating, describing and eventually manipulating light.

For this country house built in a large meadow lined with
forest, Meier drew from yet another tradition—all American
this time—that of a neo-Palladian classicism, which so much

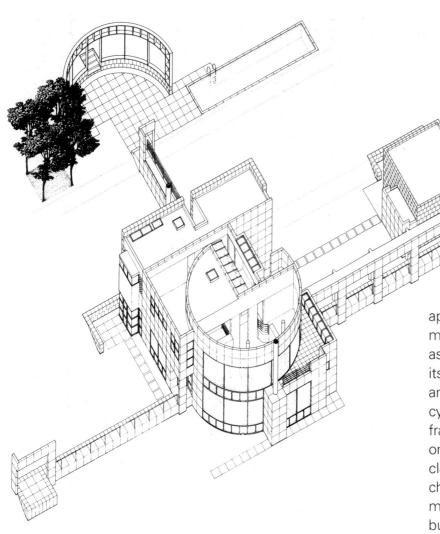

Axonometric plan of Villa
Grotta. The plan reveals
how Meier has
integrated a cylindrical
structure into a
rectangular parallelepiped.

Opposite:
An axial passageway
separates the
two bedroom wings.

Ground plan of the house.
A neo-Palladian
composition revisited,
altered by the balanced-
off-balanced design so
cherished by the Moderns.

appealed to Thomas Jefferson. The Villa Grotta is clearly a modern house with its white lacquered paneling and complex asymmetrical volumes. Its classical composition develops from its planning: three simple geometric forms, a square, a circle and a rectangle intersect, crossing into each other to form a cylindrical mass. This holds the large, double-height living room framed by a cube and a parallelepiped with the bedrooms in one part and the utility rooms in the other. The relationship to classical architecture is accentuated, not without tongue in cheek, by an arcade which leads to the entrance and has its matching piece—a free-standing arch—at the other end of the building. The opaque or glass facades are variations on the theme of the square. The view from the living room through its curved glass expanse is subdivided, interrupted by the strange-looking object of the fireplace, clad in white lacquered panels, jutting out on the exterior.

Meier intentionally chooses a narrow scope of materials and colors, from dominant white to the black wash of the living room floors and the blond wood of the parquet and the stairs. The Grotta pottery and ceramic collection, mostly of Japanese and Scandinavian origin, finds its ideal place in nature against a background of natural color. An old ceramic jar, a chair by Meis van der Rohe, or a Kwaïakult totem participate in the meeting of primitive art, handicrafts, modern architecture and landscape, a meeting that gives the Villa Grotta its little miracle of balance.

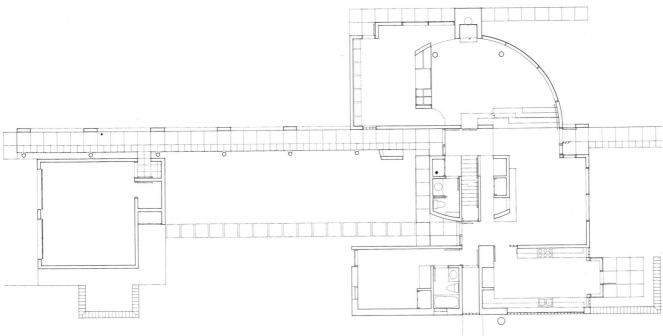

The manipulation of the
volumes and the use of
color gives the house its
monumental and classical
air.

The master bedroom curves around the landscape. Sober furnishing
with a few collector's pieces. The feline regulars at Villa Grotta.

The living room occupies part of the cylindrical structure and takes
up its full height. Wide views of the surroundings through picture
windows with, again, the theme of the square. A few pieces
of carefully-chosen furniture and pottery in earth tones, accentuating
the overall feeling of open space.

Architects' biographies

BDM ARQUITECTOS

Firm founded in Barcelona in 1972 by Briones, Dalmau and Marquez.

BRIONES, MANUEL

Born in Barcelona, 1948.
Graduated from the ETSAB in 1973.
Professor at the ETSAB (1971-1976).

DALMAU, TITO

Born in Barcelona, 1948.
Graduated from the ETSAB in 1975.
Designer of ceramics.
Winner of the First prize in design at the Cevisama '86. Participated in the International Festival of Ceramics in Tokyo, 1988.

& MARQUES, LORENZO

Born in Barcelona, 1950.
Graduated from the ETSAB in 1973.

BENEDER, ERNST

Born in Waldhofen, Austria, in 1958.
Graduated from the Technical University of Vienna (1983).
Postgraduate studies at the Tokyo Institute of Technology in 1984, 1988 and 1989.
Worked for Hans Hollein, Kazuo Shinohara and Kazunari Sakamoto.
At the same time undertook archeological digs in Turkey.
In 1987, set up his own practice in Vienna and became partners with the architect, Anja Fischer in 1996.
Guest Professor at the University of Illinois in Urbana-Champaign in 1991 and at the Technical University of Vienna from 1995 to 1996.
Winner of the Goldene Kelle Prize from the district of southern Austria in 1995.

Architectural projects:

Neuhofen Cultural Center (1994);
MegabauMax on the Laxenburgerstrasse, Vienna, with Anja Fischer (1996); a chapel and choir at Herzogenburg (1996).

BERSELLI, OTTORINO & CASSINA, CECILIA

Graduated from the University of Florence in 1982.
Based in Brescia where they have built the majority of their projects.

Works :

In Brescia: furniture shop (1985);
commercial center (1989); restructuring of the Padronale Villa (1990). Projects in construction include two residences and the renovation of two country houses, a chapel and a cemetery.

CLARE DESIGN

CLARE, LINDSAY + KERRY

Clare was born in Brisbane, Australia, 1952 and Kerry in Sydney, Australia, 1957.
Graduated from Queensland University of Technology, Australia.
Based in Buderim in Queensland.
Recipients of the National Robin Boyd Award in 1992 and 1995; the National Royal Australian Institute of Architects Commercial Award in 1995 and

the National RAIA Environment Citation 1996.

Works:

Over 60 detached houses between 1980 and 1986, including the Kinnear House (1981-1982), the Alexandra Headland House (1984-1985), the Goetz House (1984-1985) and the Thrupp and Summers House (1986-1987).

CREPAIN, JO

Born in Bruges, Belgium, in 1950.
Based in Kapellen, Belgium.
Graduated from the NHIBS of Antwerp (1973 and 1977).
Professor at the Hoger de Gand Institute of Architecture (1975-1985) and at the Henry Van de Velde Institute since 1985. Guest Professor at the Maastricht Academy in 1982, at the Rotterdam Academy from 1983 to 1984 and at the Teaching Unit of Architecture in Nantes in 1985.
Worked as a free-lance architect from 1973 to 1975, then formed a partnership with the SILO cooperative from 1975 to 1981. Set up his own practice in 1985.
Winner of the Baron Horta Prize in Architecture in 1982 and the Charles Wilford Prize in 1986 and 1991.

Works:

In Belgium: residential buildings in Etten-Leur, Apeldoorn, Nieuwland, Kattenbroek/Amersfoot; luxury appartments in Zavel/Brussels and Bolle Brug/Amersfoot. Residential buildings in Java Eiland, Amsterdam.

CZWG ARCHITECTS

London-based firm created in 1975 by four graduates of the Architectural Association School: Nick Campbell, Roger Zogolovitch, Rex Wilkinson and Piers Gough. Roger Zogolovitch left the firm in 1986.
Winner of the Royal Fine Art Commission Jeu d'esprit Award 1994.
Development and renovation of private housing in Sutton Square, Eaton Terrace, Orchard Mews, Watermint Quay, St. Paul's Mews, Camden, Rosemary Street, Islington, including development of China Wharf, Soho Lofts, etc...

Most recent works in London: the Besso House, Mile End; Royalty Studios, Notting Hill Gate; Porters Place, Smithfield; Coronation Buildings, the Vauxhall area.

GEHRY, FRANK O.

Born in Toronto, Canada, 1929.
Graduated from the University of Southern California in 1954.
Founded Frank O. Gehry Associates in 1962. Elected a Fellow of the American Institute of Architects in 1974.
Lives and works in Los Angeles.
Taught at the University of Southern California, at the University of California, Los Angeles and at Yale and Harvard.
Winner of the Pritzker Prize in 1989.

Major works:

In California: the Ron Davis studio, Malibu (1970-1972); Hollywood Bowl (1970-1982); Santa Monica Plaza (1973-1980); the main office for the Rouse Company, Columbia (1974); the Ruschka House (1977); Los Angeles Children's Museum (1979); the Gehry House, Santa Monica (1979-1987); California Aerospace Museum, Los Angeles (1982-1984); Work Residence, Beverly Hills (1982); the Norton House, Venice (1983); the Schnabel House, Brentwood (1986); the Walt Disney Concert Hall, Los Angeles (1989).
The Wintons' guest house, Wayzata, Minnesota (1984-1986); the Fish Dance restaurant, Kobe, Japan (1986-1989); the Vitra Museum, Weil am Rhein, Germany (1989); the Art Museum of the University of Minnesota (1990).

GWATHMEY, SIEGEL & ASSOCIATES ARCHITECTS

GWATHMEY, CHARLES

Attended the University of Pennsylvania School of Architecture (1956-1959). Graduated from Yale in 1962. Elected a Fellow of the American Institute of Architects in 1981.
Davenport Professor at Yale in 1983 and Bishop Professor in 1991. Guest Professor at Harvard in 1985.
Winner of the Brunner Prize 1970 from the Academy of Arts and Letters of which he became a member in 1976.
Recipient of the Medal of Honor from the New York Chapter of the AIA in 1983 and the first to receive the Yale Alumni Arts Award in 1985.

LORENZ, PETER

Born in Innsbruck, Austria, 1950.
Doctor in Architecture, Venice (1984).
Opened his Innsbruck office in 1980 and a second in Vienna in 1991.
Taught at the Univeristy of Innsbruck (1988-1990), in Salzburg (1991), and in India in 1994 at the Universities of New Delhi, Bombay and Ahmedabad.

Works:

In Innsbruck: multi-story housing complex in Peergründe (1983-1984); the Menardi House (1985-1988); the renovation and extension of the Alt-Innsbrugg Town Hall (1988-1995), the Kohlstatturm (1987-1995) and Das Triest hotel, Vienna (1991-1994).

HUNZIKER, WERNER

Born in Switzerland, 1939.
Lives and works in Luzern, Switzerland.
Worked for E. Lanter in Zurich (1960-1962).
Lived in Israel in 1962 and in Ireland in 1963.
Worked for GLC London, with Hubert Benett and with Sir L. Preston (1965-1971).
Lived in the United States between 1971 and 1973. Set up his own practice in 1973.
Solo exhibition at the Art Gallery of Meggen in 1994.

Assistant to Professor Sir L. Martin at Cambridge University from 1964 to 1965 and to Professor B. Huber at the ETH of Zurich from 1979 to 1981.
Member of the Bund Schweizer Architekten BSA in 1982.

Works:
In Switzerland: State buildings in Sempach, Meggen, Luzern and Stans, and private homes for: P. Sicher in Sempach; M. Galliker in Horw; B. Gut in Emmen and for Drs. Schibler, Beckenried, Tremp, Stans and Barmetter in Luzern.

MACK, MARK

Born in Judenburg, Austria, 1949.
Attended Technical High School in Graz and later entered the Academy of Fine Art in Vienna (1973).
Worked for Steiger & Partners in Zurich, Hans Hollein in Vienna, and for Hausrucker and Emilio Ambasz Inc. in New York (1973-1976).
In 1976, founded the Western Addition Organization in San Francisco. Formed Batey and Mack in 1978 with Andrew Batey. In 1984, set up his own firm, MACK Architects.
Professor of Architecture at the University of California, Berkeley, and at the University of California, Los Angeles since 1993.
Cofounder and editor of Archetype Magazine in 1980.
Lives and works in Venice, California.

MEIER, RICHARD & PARTNERS

MEIER, RICHARD

Born in Newark, New Jersey, 1934.
Graduated from Cornell University, Ithaca, New York (1957).
Member of the American Institute of Architects.
Established in New York.
In 1959, worked for Davis, Brody & Wisniewski, in 1960 for Skidmore, Owings & Merrill, from 1961 to 1963, for Marcel Breuer on the Whitney Museum project.
Associate Professor in Architecture at Yale University in 1975.
Winner of the Pritzker Award, 1984; Royal Gold Medal from the RIBA in 1989; honored Commander of Arts and Letters by the French government in 1992. Member of the American Academy of Arts and Sciences in 1995; AIA Gold Medal, 1997.

Major works:
Private homes: House in Essex Falls, New Jersey; Frank Stella studio, New York (1965); The Smith House, Darien, Connecticut (1967); Douglas House, Harbor Springs, Michigan (1973); Ackerberg House, Malibu, California; Grotta House, Harding Township, New Jersey (1984)...
Architectural projects:
Bronx Development Center, New York (1970); The Atheneum, New Harmony, Indiana (1975-1979); Frankfurt Museum for Decorative Arts, Frankfurt (1979); High Museum of Art, Atlanta (1980),

Getty Center, Los Angeles (1985-1992); City Hall and Central Library, The Hague (1985-1994); Cultural Center and Assembly Building, Ulm, Germany (1985-1993); Contemporary Art Museum, Barcelona (1988-1995); Weishaupt Forum, Schwendi, Germany (1992); Compaq Computers Headquarters, Houston, Texas (1994).

POOLE, GABRIEL

Australian architect, established in Doonan, Queensland.
Awarded the Gold Medal by the Royal Australian Institute of Architecture in 1998.

Major works:
Dobie Holiday House, Queensland (1972); Shubert House, Yandina (1973); Gloster House, Yandina (1983-1984) with Michael Gloster; Noble House and Gartner House, Noosa Heads (1989-1990); Mount Eerwah Tent House, Mt. Tamborine (1991)... and Gabriel & Elisabeth Poole's home and office: Lake Weyba House.

PRINCE, BART

Born in Albuquerque, New Mexico, 1947.
Assistant to Bruce Goff (1968-1973).
Set up his own practice in 1973.
Assisted Bruce Goff in building the Japanese Art Pavilion for the Los Angeles County Museum of Art, and finished the project after Goff's death.

Works:
The Bart Prince House, Albuquerque (1984); Joe Price Residence, Corona del Mar, California (1989); the Henry Whiting House, Sun Valley, Idaho (1991); the Mead/Penhall House (1992-1993); the High Residence, Mendocino County, California.

SCHNEBLI, DOLF

Born in Switzerland, 1928.
Attended the ETH of Zurich (1948-1951). Graduated from Harvard (1954).
From 1953 to 1954, worked with Daniel Girardet in Mulhouse. Instructor of Design at Harvard under Serge Chermayeff. Joined The Architects Collaborative-the Walter Gropius firm-with Serge Chermayeff and Josep Lluis Sert.
From 1957 to 1958, worked for Otto Glaus on designing the Agno Airport in Switzerland.
Set up his own practice in 1958.
In 1985, became partners with Tobias Ammann, forming a firm headed by both architects and later joined by F. Ruchat in 1991 and S. Menz in 1997: the "Sam architekten und partner AG" in Agno and Zurich.
Professor at the ETH of Zurich (1971-1994). Guest Professor at the University of Washington, at Harvard and at the University of California since 1964.

STUDIO GRANDA

HAROARDOTTIR, MARGRET

Born in Reykjavik, Iceland, 1959.

Graduated from the Architectural Association, London (1984).
In 1987, formed "Studio Granda" with Steve Christer in Reykjavik.
Vice-president of the Association of Icelandic Architects (1993-1995).
Tutor at the Architectural Association, London (1994-1995).

CHRISTER, STEVE

Born in Blackfyne, United Kingdom, 1960.
Graduated from the Architectural Association, London (1984).
Codirector of "Rafha" Architecture Workshop, Iceland (1992).
Guest Professor at the Berlage Institute, Amsterdam (1994).
Tutor at the Architectural Association, London (1994-1995).

Major works:
In Reykjavik: City Hall (1988-1992); Icelandic High Court (1994-1996); the fashion shops, Eva-Company (1994) and Galleri (1996); Reykjavik Art Museum (first prize in competition project, 1997). A number of houses in Iceland including: Pingas in Reykjavik; Birkihaed in Gardabae (1996); Tjarnamyri in Seltjarnarnes (1997); Dimmuhvarf in Kopavogur (1997); and "Aktion Poliphile" in Wiesbaden, Germany, with Ressel & Partner (1990-1992).

TURNBULL, WILLIAM ASSOCIATES

Firm created in 1970 by William Turnbull, joined by partners Mary Griffin and Eric Haesloop. Established in San Francisco, the firm is re-named "Turnbull Griffin Haesloop" in 1997 following the death of William Turnbull. From then on the firm is headed by Mary Griffin and Eric Haesloop.

TURNBULL, WILLIAM JR., FAIA

Graduated from Princeton University (1959).
From 1960 to 1963, worked for Skidmore, Owings & Merrill in San Francisco.
Founding partner of Moore, Lyndon et Whitaker in 1962.
Set up his own practice in 1970.
Member of the National Academy of Design since 1993.
Professor at Yale in 1982 and 1986.
Since 1997, Design Critic at the California College of Arts and Crafts.
Recipient of the Maybeck Award, 1993.

HAESLOOP, ERIC

Graduated from Yale (1981).
Member of the American Institute of Architects.
From 1981 to 1984, worked for Cesar Pelli & Associates in New Haven, and from 1984 to 1985 for Spencer Associates in Palo Alto. Joined William Turnbull in 1985.
Guest Critic at the University of California, Berkeley (1990-1991).
Awarded the Alpha Rho Chi Medal for Design Excellence, 1981.

Works:
In California: Spencer Residence,

Oakville; Anderson Residence, Sea Ranch; Walters Residence, Mendocino and Trowbridge Residence, Orinda; Brown Street Apartments, St. Helena; Mountain View City Hall and Community Theater, Mountain View. Regent Hotel, Singapore.

VASQUEZ CONSUEGRA, GUILLERMO

Born in Seville, 1945.
Graduated from the ETSAS (1972).
Professor at the ETSAS from 1972 to 1975 and 1980 to 1987.
Guest Professor at the Faculty of Architecture and Urban Studies of Buenos Aires in 1993 and at the Federal Polytechnic School of Lausanne in 1995.
Visiting Scholar at the Getty Center, Los Angeles, 1994 to 1995.
Recipient of the First Prize, the Order of Architects, in 1988, 1991 and 1992 and the Construmat Prize in 1989.

Major works:
In Seville: the Rolando House (1980); the Andalusian Government Headquarters (1992), the Navigation Pavilion for the Expo' 92; the Andalusian Heritage Insitute (1990-1995); low-income housing in Seville (1984), Cadiz (1986), Madrid (1987) and Almendralejo (1988); the Telefonica building in Seville (1992) and Cadiz (1993).

Bibliography

American House. New Contemporary Architectural Design, Thames & Hudson, 1997.
American Masterworks. The Twentieth Century House, Rizzoli, New York, 1995.
L'Architecture espagnole contemporaine. Les Années 80, Gustavo Gili ed., Barcelona, 1991.
Country Houses, Axis Books, Barcelona, 1995.
Graham Jahn, *Contemporary Australian Architecture*, ed. Gordon and Breach Arts International, 1994.
Grands architectes et maisons américaines du xxᵉsiècle, Le Seuil, Paris, 1995.
Modern American Houses. Four Decades of Award-Winning Design in Architectural Design, Harry N. Abrams Inc./Architectural Record, 1992.
Philip Jodicio, *Contemporary American Architects*, Benedikt Taschen, 1996.
Arnell Peter & Bickford Ted, *Frank Gehry, buildings and projetcs*, Rizzoli, New York, 1985.
Philip Jodicio, *Richard Meier*, Benedikt Taschen, 1995.

Photo credits

Pages 40 to 47, 102 to 109: Reiner Blunck
Back cover, pages 8 to 15, 48 to 55, 118 to 125: Richard Bryant / Arcaid
Pages 62 to 69: Luis Casals
Pages 94 to 101: Tito Dalmau
Pages 70 to 77: Mark Darley/Esto Photographics Inc.
Pages 150 to 157: Scott Frances/Esto Photographics Inc.
Pages 56 to 61: Giancarlo Gardin
Pages 134 to 141: Christopher Irion
Pages 142 to 149: Peter Kopp
Pages 110 to 117: Lucinda Lambton
Pages 126 to 133: Norbert Migueletz
Pages 32 to 39: Alberto Piovano
Pages 86 to 93: George Seper, Terry Straight, Richard Stringer
Pages 16 to 23: Margherida Spilutini
Front cover: Telleri
Pages 78 to 85: Paul Warchol
Pages 24 to 31: A. Zimmermann

Printed in Italy